Universal Harmony

Universal Harmony

S. H. Munzig

ISBN 978-0-6151-5616-3

Cover, Art and Graphics
by
Scott Munzig

Original Paintings and Prints
available at
Banana Patch Studio
P.O. Box 950
Hanapepe, Hawaii 96716

See Painting Images at:
www.bananapatchstudio.com

California Representative:
Patricia Johnson
www.helenskylar@aol.com

Dedicated
To The Memory of My Brother

David "Dirtz" Munzig

Whose visit upon this earth was brief,
yet his example of living,
independent of opinion,
in the manner he chose,
will be remembered
forever
by those
who were fortunate enough
to have known him.

Some Words of Thanks

I should mention, before beginning this book, that it was never my intention it become a book at all, nor did the words within come about through any extraordinary effort on my part. There was, however, considerable work done in the editing and arrangement of the manuscript's pages. This came through the patience of my father.

It is also of importance to acknowledge the Illuminated Souls who were instrumental in putting my feet upon the Path to Realization. Mahalo to a Beautiful Expression of God's Love, Rev. Dianne Winter, an international spiritual counselor and teacher of the celebrated philosophy of the Science of Mind as well as other metaphysical philosophies. To another great teacher in my life, who chooses to remain anonymous, I give my heartfelt thanks for his guidance and the many gifts along the way. And, I would be remiss not to mention my long-time comrade Janet, for her stern but loving support through the many years that we were together.

Many blessings to my family, friends and acquaintances who are not mentioned in these pages, but who know that they, too, are part of me

Author's Introduction

My choice of words within the pages to come are limited. I do not know a great deal of philosophical or intellectual words. I do not feel, however, they are appropriate. The Truth is simple; it's not necessary to muck it up with a bunch of sophisticated terminology. On the following pages many of the same words in my descriptions are used repeatedly throughout the introduction and especially into the core, the bulk of the book itself.

It would be beneficial to the reader to point out here that my use of the words Spirit, Mind, Soul, God, Intelligence, Thought, Principle, Self, Consciousness, Energy, *etc*. I use only for the purpose of explanation as to *how Creation works*; for, in the context of this book, they represent the same thing.

Although much of the wording and content within these statements appear similar, their meaning may be overlooked by the reader. By reformulating these words and restructuring their sentences, it is my intention that in so doing, I may approach the message within them from a slightly difference angle. In this way it is my hope that one of the messages that may have been overlooked earlier will strike a keynote within the Conscious Soul and spring forth into Recognition.

While the majority of these statements are apparent on the surface, many require a great deal of contemplation/meditation for the Light of their Truth to break over you. Once understood, each one can lead to the translation of the other and help quicken your imagination to finer points of reasoning.

To add further clarification, you will find that some of the wording in *Universal Harmony* may seem incomprehensible, but it is certainly not my intention to

1

confound anyone. Reason and logic are not enough to "see" the Truth that I'm hinting at within such wording. Thinking processes alone are insufficient, for the Truth is constantly moving through the moment, constantly undergoing a transformation. To catch a glimpse of that which Is, patience and openness of mind are essential. So I ask that you not dismiss those "statements" which, at first glance, appear difficult to understand; for I assure you, there is a significance behind each. What their significance is, however, must be up to each reader to determine and the depth of their meaning can only be measured according to the degree of individual Comprehension/Realization.

The ideas from which these statements were born are universal. In other words, you already know their meaning. They are just beneath your conscious mind. It is only a matter of allowing the Truth within them to come to the surface without any force of effort. May I suggest that you read them slowly and as many times as necessary. Go back to them again and again, as Comprehension is usually found when one is best prepared to Know.

This is not to imply that one will not benefit without full comprehension of this book's material, for even when the analytical mind of man fails to fathom the meaning behind the words it's reading, the Conscious Soul, the Real "witness," has absolute cognition of the Truth. That is to say, when Soul "witnesses" Truth, It recognizes Itself. The core of man's being can be jumping for joy in rapturous recognition while the outer man, although definitely feeling a sense of "upliftment," may remain unaware as to the reason why. Therefore, the very reading of these pages should be beneficial and influential toward initiating an Awakening within the human vehicle.

My initial inspiration for this writing came to me after Awakening from the most problematic period of my life, that of internal conflict, discontent, and drug dependence. These blessings, although beyond my grasp to recognize them at the time, culminated in an arrest for drug possession. It was shortly thereafter that my entire perception of the world changed.

Approximately six months following my arrest, while lying on the cold concrete floor in a hot prison cell on the island of Maui, I inadvertently relaxed into an attentive, yet deep, state of meditation. I found myself, as consciousness, gazing into a vast bowl of empty space. This I recognized as timelessness, something I had been pondering for years prior to this experience.

Superimposed on this timeless space came what appeared to be a thundercloud; it seemed to be aware, alive, manifesting from within itself the instant that it came into contact with the timelessness. I, as conscious, recognized the cloud as a representation of thought, of mind.

It was HERE, in an indescribable jolt of illumination, that comprehension unfolded instantanously. In a flash of impersonalized Realization I "saw" both the beginning and end of all things seen and unseen in Unison. At that moment "I" was no longer gazing at this Phenomenon from the perspective of a witness, but was the Phenomenon Itself.

There was no sense of separation or "otherness," just the silent awareness of a perpetual state of *Being*. Within an exquisite and nostalgic impression of Completeness, I, as Being, at once KNEW this was, and is, the very Principle of Existence, the Cause, the very Reason we ARE. What was felt not only explained the nature of Stillness, but how this potential spirit, or "ISness," was imaged forth as manifestation when influenced by mind; a continuous *coming into being* within a flowing succession of moments.......always NOW.

After this experience, in elated Astonishment, I felt as if I had just discovered an ancient secret, something that I had always known, but had been lingering just beyond my conscious grasp. So overwhelmed with joyous emotion was I, that both tears and laughter welled up from my heart. I noticed that the tension, which for so many years I had been holding inside, was released in what felt like endless exhilaration. For the first time in my life my breathing became deep, effortless and rhythmic. The very air within my prison cell seemed to have been transformed into something other than air itself; something soft, soothing, charged like a light humming with vibrant energy. This penetrated and permeated not only everything that surrounded me, but mingled with every fiber of my being. It ignited my conscious awareness which became magnified with the lucidity that I had never experienced before.

Although what I write now is coherent, I found it nearly impossible to translate or verbalize the initial experience: How this Principle "works" or how It converts Timelessness into time.

In the days that followed, I realized that anything I put to contemplation, when seen in the light of this Unitary Principle, became intuitively clear and obvious. It was like a knife unseen had cut a hole in the fabric of time, a portal through which I could "look" beyond the net of the thought-bound mind.

In awe of these wondrous revelations, I spent a few sleepless nights examining the gravity and implications of what all this meant. All the while, without any conscious intent, much of my life's hypnotic conditioning of ill-conceived ideas, concepts, perceptions and long-held beliefs began to passively slip away of their own accord.

Eventually and quite humbly, I settled back into my meditations. These, in turn, resulted in many tangible and richly illuminating experiences that came in the form of what I could only term as *untarnished inner feelings.* With eager curiosity I was prompted to evaluate the validity of these feelings and write them down as nearly as I could interpret. I simply began to call these short passages, "Statements."

I started writing as a means of integrating their meaning into fuller comprehension; to capsulate them in order to hold the meaning of these feelings within the memory. After having sent portions of this writing to my father, he suggested that it be shared. It was here that the idea for the book came into being, encompassing the variety of perspectives it was to contain.

The inspired "Statements" were fashioned from the background of understanding gained through the major influences of my Awakened life. The words of Paul Twitchell, Emma Curtis Hopkins, Earnest Holms, Kirpal (Sudar) Singh, Krishnamurti and Carlos Castaneda are integrated within many of these pages.

What the reader may come to see, without much cognizant application, is that behind the formulation of this book are many diverse ideas and, as you may also come to see, ideas themselves can only be derived from other ideas.

Yet, are not the origin of all ideas born of God? There is nothing original within this world; no one can claim any idea as his own for they belong to the Universe, the source from which they arose. Ideas concerning Truth can only be expressed in so many ways. The Truth is One and there are but a few ways to attempt to frame it.

This is why so many arrive at the same conclusions independently of one another. All ideas about the Truth eventually lead back to the Original Idea as they must conform to, and surround their Singular Origin.

Is it no wonder that all spiritual writings are similar regardless of their author? The only difference being not in their conclusions or their attempt to give it, but in their choice of words and placement of them, in their effort to convey it.

Through this effort of conveyance it is my sincere hope that if what you read and study in *Universal Harmony* brings just a little light, understanding and harmony into the life of you, the reader, this book will have served its purpose.

I lay no claim to being either "the author" or "the artist." I am merely a conduit through which Beauty has found expression. This is true for all of us. Take your time with the Statements that follow. Relax, be still and read slowly. May your life's Quest be complete.

Scott Munzig

Universal Harmony

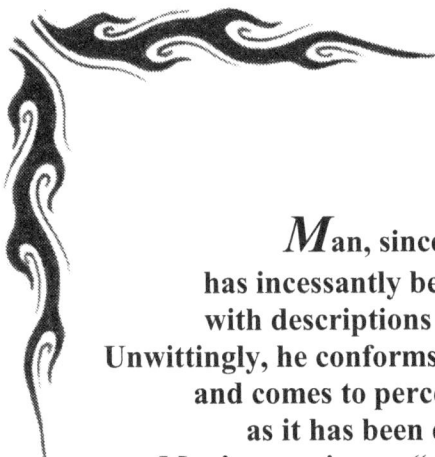

*M*an, since birth,
has incessantly been presented
with descriptions of the world.
Unwittingly, he conforms to such descriptions
and comes to perceive the world
as it has been described.
Man's experiences "seem" to validate
the authenticity of the descriptions
by those who had originally described them;
therefore, nothing is questioned
and the cycle is perpetuated.
In this manner humanity, as a whole,
conforms to a common belief,
a common "interpretation" of the world of Reality.
In truth, this is nothing more
than the most subtle form of hypnotism;
herein lies the reason so few glimpse outside
this illusionary flow of perception.
To break the chains of this dogmatic conformity
is to discover Reality;
to see not descriptions and interpretations
of what we have *learned* to perceive Reality to be,
but to look beyond the veil of interpretation ---
to witness the world,
as it IS.

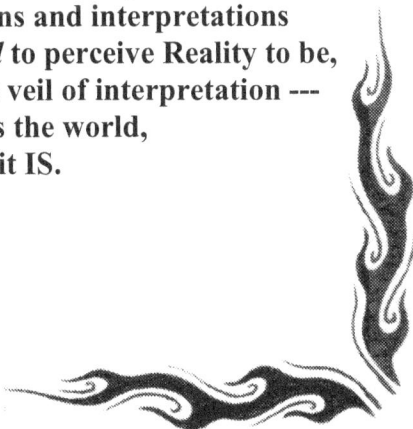

*G*od is not the creator of words,
descriptions or concepts.
These are man's *ideas*
which God knows nothing of.
Concepts *about* Creation
are entirely *man's creation*.
It is "we"
who give illusionary meaning to our ideas,
our concepts about Reality,
then, foolishly believe they *have meaning*.
As an example:
There never was, nor will there ever be,
a thing call disharmony,
unless, of course,
what we *believe*
disharmony to mean.

*T*he True state of man's Being
is like a Gem
covered with many layers of dirt.
It lies buried under the rubble
of the conditioned mind.
It is always *There* ---
we need only to strip away the
accumulated impressions of false belief
to find It, as It, has always been.
We need not entirely forget
our learned impressions,
but more importantly,
remember who and what we were
before they were pressed in
upon us.

*B*y giving names and labels to things,
the observer quickly dismisses them
thinking he has understood,
yet he understands not at all.
The moment one labels anything,
his observation has ceased.
The essence of the thing observed
is lost to the observer.
Without seeking to identify,
to translate ---
through naming,
through labeling -
one is compelled to *look,*
and by *looking,*
one comprehends things
as they ARE.

*F*rom it's bases in accumulated knowledge,
the mind quickly compares,
analyzes and judges
what it looks upon.
Through this process,
this screen of resistance,
man rarely sees things as they *Are*,
but sees only *his beliefs*
about them.

Let go your ideas of the world,
for it is nothing more
than the imagination
of men.
Strip away all beliefs
and there is found,
what IS.

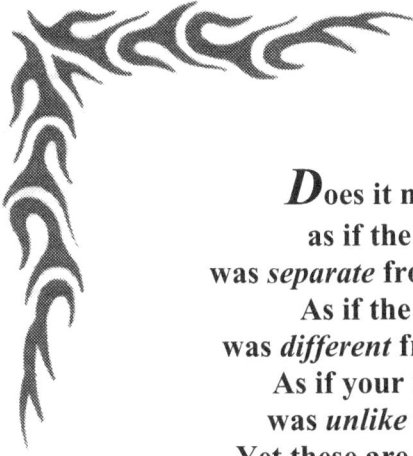

*D*oes it not seem
as if the ocean
was *separate* from the shore?
As if the flower
was *different* from the soil?
As if your neighbor
was *unlike* yourself?
Yet these are differences,
where in fact,
none exists.
Man is so accustomed, so hypnotized
from gazing at form and capacity
that he fails to fathom
the Unity
of all things.
We needn't judge according to appearances,
but *imagine* their Spiritual essence
coming into view.
We needn't separate the varying forms of the earth,
but *visualize* their intermingling sameness
occupying the places that differences claim to be.
It is through such imagination,
such visualization,
that Unity comes to be "seen."
Ever-expanding,
imagery perceives the Actual.
Ever-widening,
vision apprehends the Real.

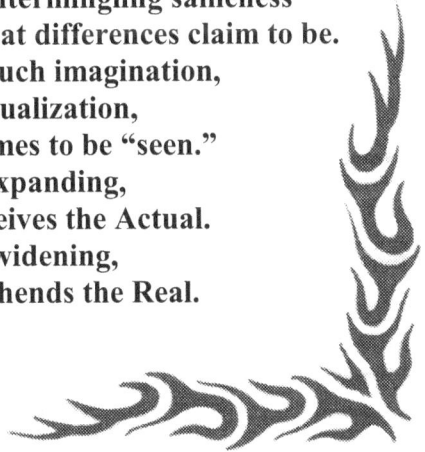

*I*f man feels isolated,
insignificant or alone,
he is but forgetful
of his *True Estate*,
unknowing,
of his Unity with Creation.
This and this alone,
is the source
of his confusion.

*I*mperfection exists only in the "seeming."
Consciously or unconsciously,
every adverse aspect of your Nature
has appeared in the form of your belief.
Your Nature,
however,
is God,
who's eyes do not behold iniquity.
Imperfection *is* perfection
when seen
in the Glorious Light of Truth.
Believe in this
and the "seeming" will vanish
into airy
nothingness.

*A*s the trend of all life in the Universe,
we are evolving
as a manifest species.
A mutation through necessity,
toward the greater expression
of the Inner Spirit.
Not a *becoming,*
but an Awakening
from the *inner,*
transforming
the *outer.*

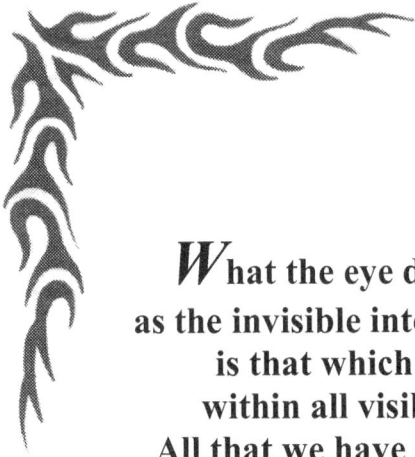

*W*hat the eye does not detect
as the invisible intelligence of God,
is that which hides itself
within all visible creation.
All that we have come to regard
as solid matter,
is,
in Reality,
the emptiness
of Spirit in Form.
Every particle in existence
is not only wrapped
within the emptiness of intelligence,
but is saturated
by the Wisdom of a Spiritual Atmosphere.
Truly, the tapestry of creation
is the non-solidified essence
of Spirit,
appearing as the shadows of matter,
woven together,
by the threads of Mind.(2)

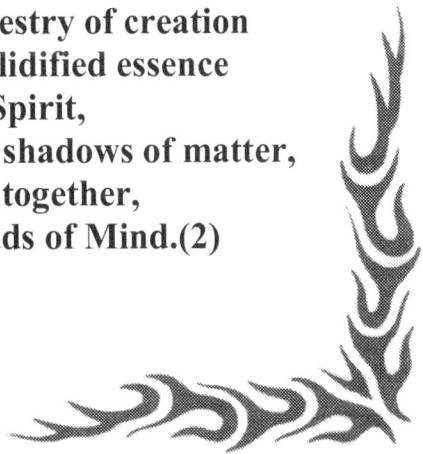

*W*rapped within a purposeful design
of mutual evolution,
every star in the firmament
and every soul that dwells therein
did not appear separately,
nor subsequently,
but were imaged forth
in the same instant,
in the same way,
for the same purpose
of returning as the same Equalibrium
as the Original Design.

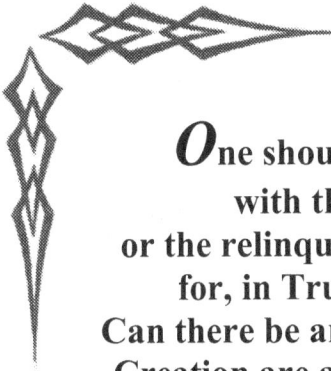

*O*ne should not be concerned
with the dissolvement,
or the relinquishment of the ego-self;
for, in Truth, it never existed.
Can there be an ego where Creator and
Creation are a singular phenomenon?
There is not God and something less.
To reason in any other manner would be
to strengthen and fix one's belief in separation;
hence, to remain "reaching" for the realm of
Reality.
Look, there is nothing *other* than the Self.
Self is synonymous with God,
the *Omnipresent*.
Other than this,
there is only the imagination,
the outer formulation,
as the shroud around the God Self,
that which we have come to believe ourselves to be.
There never was,
nor will there ever be,
an ego to dissolve, to relinquish,
save the projection of the mind,
the thought, the emotion, the idea,
the false impressions,
of the illusionary,
"me."

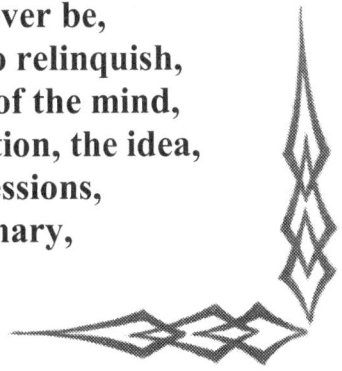

*G*od is but a single word
to describe Everything
both visible and invisible.
There is not you, me *and* God
in all the Universe.
That which seems separate is,
in fact,
at once,
the same *Thing*.

*S*pirit is synonymous with God.
We are as much of IT
as we Know we are.
It is this: Spirit, as Cause, is Knowing;
Spirit, as Effect, is Being;
therefore, to Know,
is to BE.
They are One in the Same
as the Unity of a Self-fulfilling Law.
This principle of Spirit is not something
one grasps at
for there is no element of time.
You *are* That,
within a flowing succession of moments,
immersed in a stream of existence,
as the continuum of Now.

*T*he Essence,
the Creative Substance of the Universe,
eagerly awaits
the direction of the Conscious Soul;
for they have but One Will and Desire,
to express as the Love
they Know themselves,
to BE.

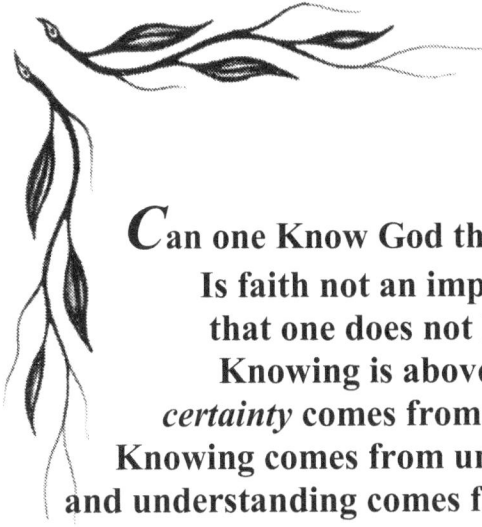

*C*an one Know God through faith?
Is faith not an implication
that one does not Know?
Knowing is above faith,
certainty comes from Knowing,
Knowing comes from understanding,
and understanding comes from certainty ---
that of Knowing you *will* understand.
In this manner one must come to Know,
the Known,
for man is the Knower
and God is the Known,
the Knower and the Known are One.
Some feel they need faith as a "bridge"
to span an imaginary gap
between man
and the Shore of the Eternal.
The Knower needs no such "tool;"
he stands on that Shore Now,
One,
with the Shore Itself.

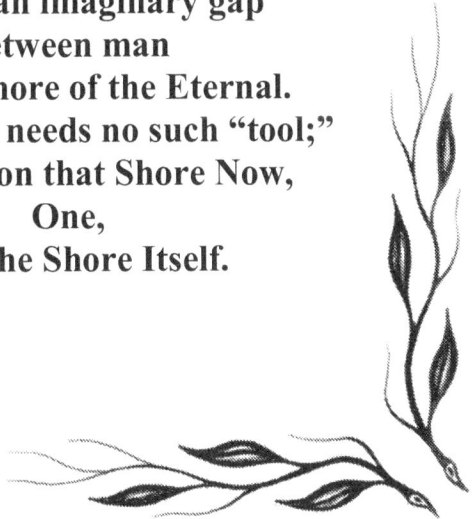

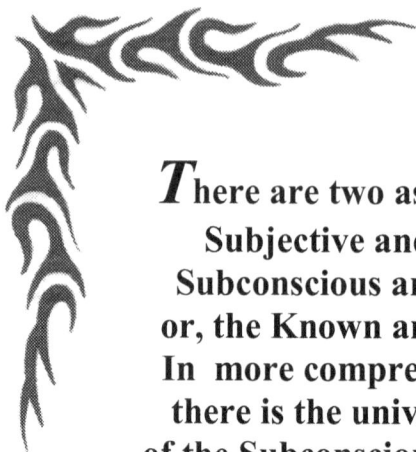

*T*here are two aspects of Mind:
Subjective and Objective,
Subconscious and Conscious;
or, the Known and the *Knower*.
In more comprehensive terms,
there is the universal memory
of the Subconscious mind of man,
and the clear Awareness
of the Conscious Mind of God,
in man.
Understanding this,
the seeker
is brought to a point of discovery,
a Realization of facts pertaining to his
True Nature.
Yet these are but indications
of the gateway to Illumination,
this being,
Mind,
encompassing It's other half.
For it is *there*,
in the instant
of It's Eternal Self-comprehension,
that the two,
Awaken,
as *ONE*.

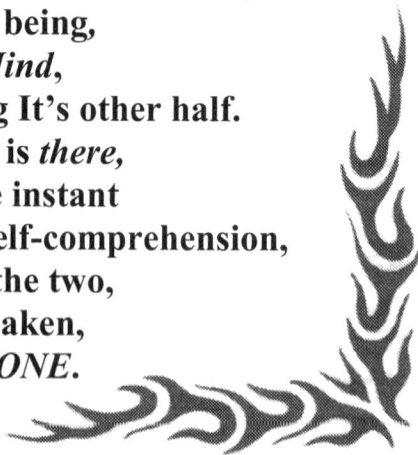

*M*an,
as Soul,
could not learn the value of *each* life
if he were born with memory,
the prejudices, likes and dislikes
of *former* life.
With an accumulation
of all Knowledge acquired,
through every experience
which he has passed,
Man,
in his finite consciousness,
would be overwhelmed by such infinitude.
Yet if one be Spiritually fit
and transcends himself;
when he,
the Knower,
Awakens to the Known,
then Soul's experiences throughout Creation,
and the Wisdom therefrom
would be revealed,
laid out like stars aligned,
spanning Eternity.

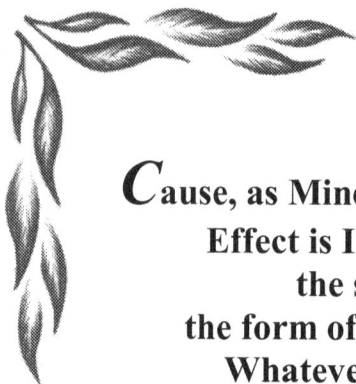

*C*ause, as Mind, as God, is BELIEF.
Effect is IT's appearance,
the substance,
the form of what is Believed.
Whatever one Believes,
it must come forth into visible expression.
Regardless the appearance or the outcome,
it is always God
in the form of BELIEF.(1)
We have heretofore been unaware of the Law,
this Principle of Creation ---
We must now *Know;*
It is done (manifests) unto you as you BELIEVE.
As much of God you can conceive,
you can BE;
for *"as"* the Mind of God,
man,
Believing,
can embody all IT IS.
Man,
Awakened to this Truth,
is not just a Knower of Truth,
but encompassing the Truth,
he IS
the *Truth Itself.*

*I*f one is seeking at all,
Knowingly or not,
he is seeking God.
Yet that which seeks
was never separate
from the object of the search.
Since you seek God,
it would only be appropriate,
that you introduce yourself,
to Yourself.

*T*here is a *H*armony of *P*erfection
pervading all Creation.
"Thy Kingdom Has Come."
When you *believe* it,
you will see it.
Not the other way around.

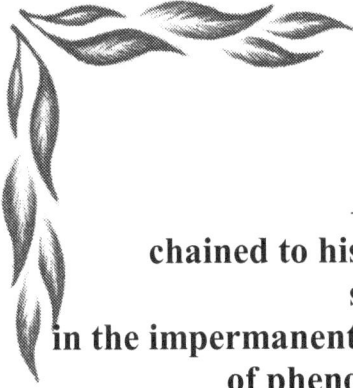

*M*an,
chained to his desire for security,
seeks it
in the impermanent and illusionary character
of phenomenal objects.
Once the false impetus for such desire is found,
man sees his error
and is delivered out of the bonds
of his misguided approach.
No longer seeking in the phenomenal world,
man begins to look *within.*
Here, eradicated of his worldly
and cumulative ambition,
the impelling force of his desire,
like a flame,
dies,
for lack of fuel.
Relinquished of the bonds of this incessant reflex,
man,
laboriously,
steps closer,
to
Utter Freedom.

*W*ithout a leap of faith,
God proves Itself.
Through simple observation,
one can easily see an Intelligence operating
through Everything.
Such Intelligence is self-evident.
It is self-evident in your own being.
If one were to say,
"I need proof of God,"
would be as if to say,
one needs proof
of his own existence.

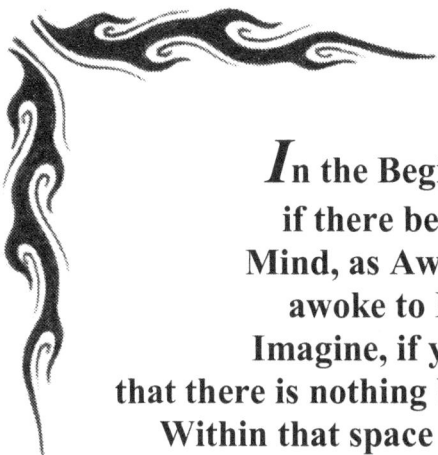

*I*n the Beginning,
if there be such,
Mind, as Awareness,
awoke to Itself.
Imagine, if you will,
that there is nothing but empty space.
Within that space is Awareness.
Now,
there being nothing but empty space,
what is there
for this awareness
to be aware of?
Awareness, in its silent contemplation,
can only find Itself to be
the very Awareness that is Aware.
Here, in a burst of miraculous
Self-Recognition,
Awareness awakens to *Itself,*
endlessly proclaiming:
I-Am, I-Am, I-Am.
Or as the Sage puts it, OMM.
It is this same *continual* Self-Recognition
that brings forth all things
from the God-center within themselves.
The Self Existent Principle of
All that IS.

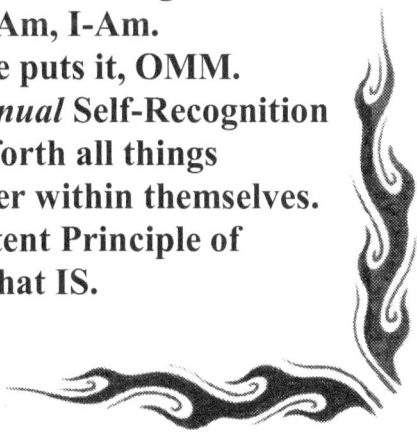

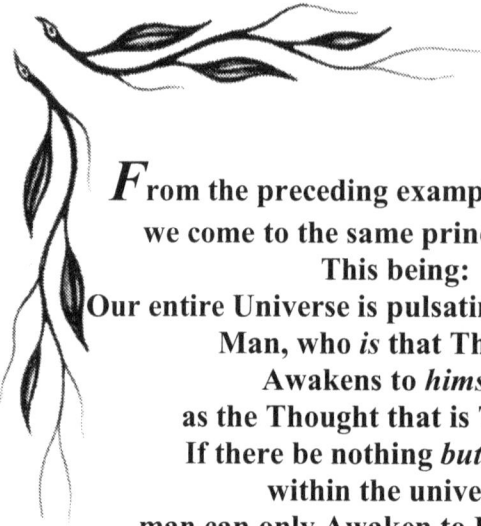

*F*rom the preceding example of awareness
we come to the same principle in man.
This being:
Our entire Universe is pulsating with Thought.
Man, who *is* that Thought,
Awakens to *himself,*
as the Thought that is Thinking.
If there be nothing *but* Thought
within the universe
man can only Awaken to It, as *himself,*
the Thought which he IS.
Man, as Thought,
unsolidified as "the potential"
recognizes *himself*
and solidifies as "manifestation."
Moving upon itself,
Thought *continually awakens* ,
Self-Recognition,
instantaneously repeating,
giving birth to *itself* out of itself.
This principle is rarely discerned,
for it is an unconscious process
just as thought;
yet, the very fact that you *are* thought,
is the Self-explanation
of your Being.

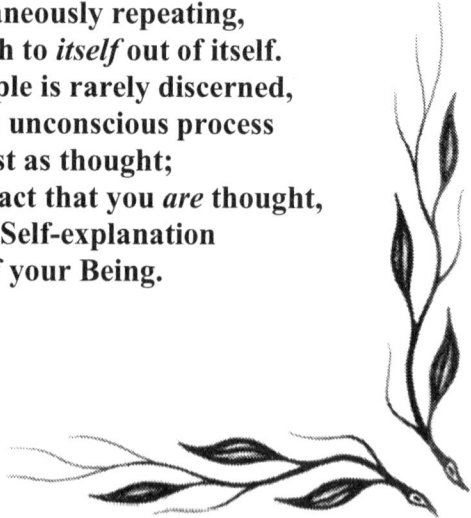

*M*ind, the foundation of the Universe,
thinks all things into existence.
Thought moves outward
then back upon Itself
in a perpetual process of Self Recognition.
It sustains Itself in each instant
through a continual Realization of
That which It Is.
Your Being is a thought,
at once ONE with Divine Mind
which is able to perpetuate itself,
by knowing Itself,
as the thought which It Is.(6)
To realize this Principle,
is to realize the Mystery
behind all Mysteries.

*T*he thought,
the thinker
and
the thing thought about,
are all the same in Being.
This Being *is* all there is.
Consequently, IT IS whatever
It thinks it is,
in the instant
of Its thinking.

*M*an's experience *is* whatever
he introduces to his Consciousness,
even at the most subtle levels.
Man's words always reveal themselves
in the world around him.
Therefore, one should never say anything
he does not want to see
Realized in his life.

*M*an mistakes the
Universal Intelligence of Mind
for the sensory recording instrument
of the human brain.
The brain is but an electrically impulsed machine,
used to ascertain, assimilate,
and compare all things of the senses
in this sensory world.
It is a storehouse for memory,
which has no motivating intelligence,
in and of itself.
The brain, in man,
is akin to an antenna
that picks up the impress of Universal Mind
from outside the physical form.
This Mind is what man calls space.
It alone is intelligence.
The motivating Force that creates,
stimulates, and sustains the life
within the human vehicle
through its short span
of earthly existence;
then,
into the existences beyond.

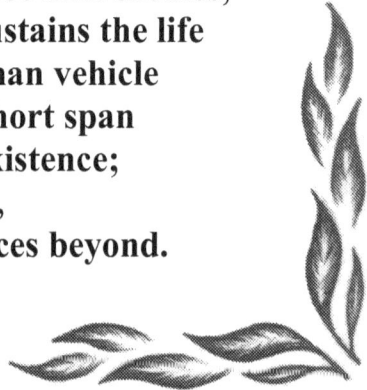

*F*rom the Stillness of Being,
mind "thinks" in one of two directions:
Past (memory)
or future (anticipation).
When the mind is stilled,
between these two,
there
Reality resides ---
in the Eternal Now,
the Uncreated,
the Undifferentiated
and choiceless Awareness,
of the Absolute.

*T*here is a crack
between the two foundations
of the universe.
They are: Positive and negative or
reality and illusion.
Forget them both.
Neither one will lead to Truth
as they are open to
the mind's speculation,
conjecture and interpretation.
Jump through the crack between them.
Only then may you look back
on the foundation
you were once within,
but no longer of.

*T*he cat that chases the mouse;
the infant reaching for her mother;
the insect crawling at your feet;
the intruder who kills.
All are compelled by the same desire even
though their motivations *appear* different.
If one is honest,
one can find a commonality
with all the above,
a thread of Unity
running *through* each,
and *to* which we are all drawn.(2)
Every action we take,
every movement we make,
is to bring something to ourselves.
It is to further the goodness, the "Godness,"
That we are all
unconsciously seeking.

*I*f one knows no comparisons,
there is no reference point
from which to judge.
God is *all* ---
you cannot compare
that
which *is*
Everything
to
Everything.

*R*ealizing Spirit is *All,*
our former ideas of the world
all fall to pieces;
with nothing left
to support their claim of reality,
they evaporate
under the hot sun of Truth.

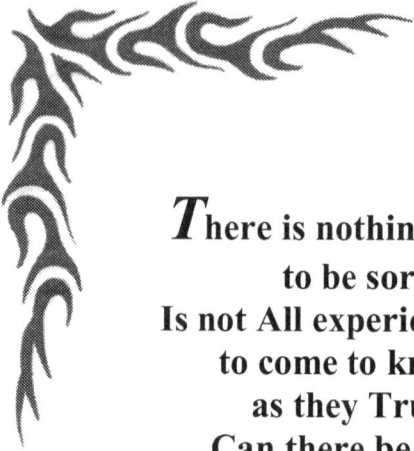

*T*here is nothing in the world
to be sorry for.
Is not All experience necessary
to come to know things
as they Truly Are?
Can there be mountains
without valleys?
Victory without a battle?
Can you know light
without it's opposite in contrast?
One cannot Know Peace
without suffering,
or joy without sorrow.
There must also be the descent
of ignorance
in order to comprehend the ascent
into Enlightenment.
All experience, then,
without exception,
is appropriate,
necessary,
and Perfect.

*T*ears of joy are awaiting
the one who discovers;
there are no mistakes.
Everything you did,
needed to be done.

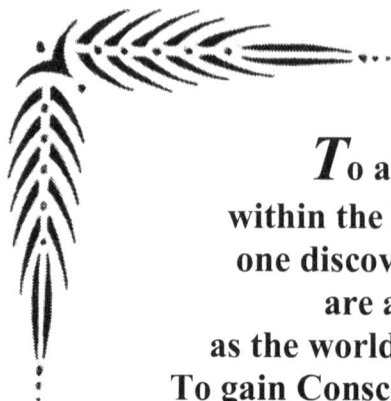

*T*o awaken,
within the Dreamstate,
one discovers Dreams
are as real
as the world around him.
To gain Conscious Awareness,
within the Dreamstate,
one learns he can control
the course of the Dream.
The visible world and
the invisible world of Dreaming,
are products of a Single Mind.
Therefore,
if man can Consciously control his Dreams,
he is controlling the Only Mind there is.
It then follows,
that when man Knows himself as the Mind,
he Knows himself as the Dreamer,
in control,
of the Life he Dreams.
Within such Realization,
he may now take Conscious
and Pragmatic Control
of his Self-created World
and the Forces,
Known as God.

*T*his worldly show,
this Grand Illusion,
has taken place in a dream world.
Now Awake,
I walk through the dream,
aware of the fact that I am dreaming,
shaping the dream to my choosing.

*W*hat is there for one to hope for?
Does not hoping imply
that there is something
within one's nature
as yet unfulfilled?
Put away your hope, and *Know:*
"The life of thy Self
is the completed splendor
of the Victorious Unseen."
There is nothing to Become,
there is nothing to Overcome.
All is *here,*
Now.

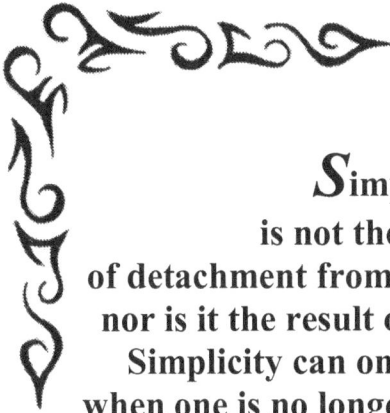

*S*implicity
is not the outcome
of detachment from worldly possessions;
nor is it the result of virtue or practice.
Simplicity can only come into being
when one is no longer pursuing anything.
One who is without compulsion,
or need of direction,
is through with all such complex processes,
the pressures of *becoming.*
When one's interest
is no longer fixed on change,
he comes into an inner sense
of calm and surrender.
Such a one relinquishes all effort,
becomes poised, relaxed, tranquil,
and enters contentment,
a contentment,
that only comes
through the end of the pursuit,
which is the Acceptance,
the Simplicity,
of life
as it IS.

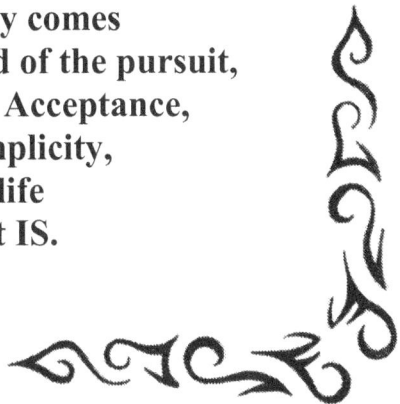

*L*ife itself is not influencing us
to experience either
joy or sadness.
It is, however,
attempting to teach us to accept
the beauty of what IS;
the simplicity of
moment to moment
existence.
Joy or sadness arise as
either success or failure
in embracing this
Life Teaching.

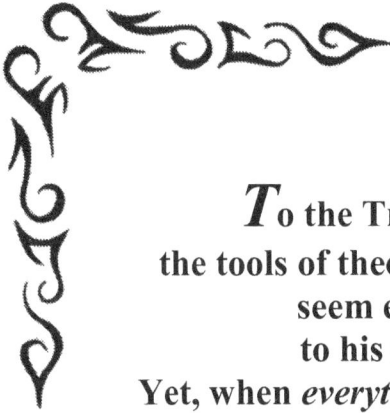

*T*o the Truth seeker
the tools of theory and analyses
seem essential
to his search.
Yet, when *everything* is seen as the
same thing,
then what is left to analyze?
You see, once the Unitary Fact
of existence is ascertained;
once the seer *sees* that neither *himself*,
nor any objective theory,
has any independent existence
apart from the Mind
in which they originated,
then all such tools are discarded.
Here, in the blink of an eye,
the grand enigma dissolves
into the twilight of Clear Perception.
Eternity's gates then begin to swing open
as the analyzer and the analyzed
merge into an unending communion
of transcendental
at-one-ment.

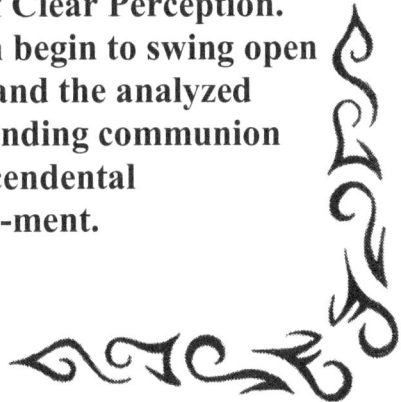

Nothing exists save in connection
with an onlooker.
Would the Universe exist without "*I*"
to perceive it?
Can "*I*" be removed
from the whole of consciousness?
Adjust thy perception
to the Universal Sameness,
and IT's *Power* is with thee.

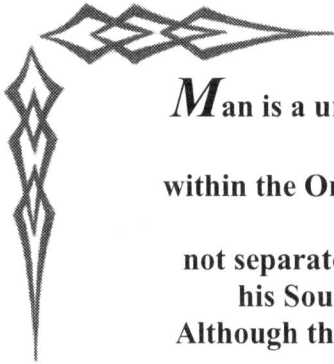

*M*an is a unique and individualized point
of consciousness
within the One Overdwelling Consciousness
of the Universe;
not separated from, but United with this,
his Source of all Creative Power.
Although the Overdwelling Consciousness
is Intelligence,
It has no volition of Its own.
It knows only how to respond, to work,
to bring forth into expression,
whatever is impressed upon It.
Always obedient,
in accordance to man's consciousness,
It acts upon his thoughts,
whatever those thoughts may be.
This is God In Action,
working at the level of individual consciousness.
In understanding this,
each individual may unlock his secret powers
to create the freedom,
he has so fervently sought;
for man, as the conscious thinker,
learning how to think,
can reshape his mind, his environment,
and everything within it.
Man, as the Maker, Remakes;
He, as the Molder, Remolds,
dispelling all unpleasantness,
neutralizing all error.(1)
He is *his own Savior* --- the Creator
of the Destiny he chooses.

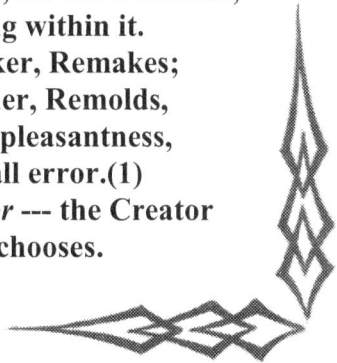

*L*imitation
is a word devoid of meaning.
Limitless thoughts
leaves one open
to limitless possibilities:
The unprecedented,
the unbelievable,
the unexpected.

*M*an, believing his body to be Real,
mistakes his True Nature
to be that
which is *seen,*
and therefore,
believes he can be abused and insulted.
Yet the *True Man* is not the body;
the *Spirit-self* cannot be *seen.*
What, then, is there to abuse?
How can *it* be insulted?

*T*here can be no suffering,
no insult, no injury,
Knowing
that all that is manifest
is but the outpicturing
of the thought behind it.
Matter is not but a thought,
and how can a thought
injure a thought?

*A*ll life has but a single lineage,
though the temporary vehicles,
which we inherit,
seem separated by time,
space and appearance.
Past Conscious Life
is the *same* Conscious Life,
Here and Now.
There is but a single stream of Consciousness,
inseparable from the vehicles
of It's former inhabitation.
To follow this line of reasoning
is to see,
that the implication here must be,
that we,
as Conscious Life,
are our own forefathers.

*T*here is but One,
Self-existent Reality
forever Creating Itself,
out of Itself,(1)
by Itself,
forever remaining Itself,
and Is everything
It Creates.

"*L*ook to the Lillies of the Field,
they toil not,
nor do they spin."
What is meant by this?
Why are we told to Look?
Clearly it points to
the simplicity of nature,
its absence of impediments
and uncertainty.
Plants do not question their *Being* ---
they are not stifled with concern,
that of becoming,
of attainment,
all this mattering of existence.
Plants, as conscious intelligence,
through the natural perpetuation
of harmony,
remain in a passive state of tranquility.
They simply *Know* they are,
therefore,
they *Are.*
Effortlessly, loving themselves
into existence
they come forth beautiful.
Look ---
what a tremendous example!

"*T*ake no Thought"
For knowing one is Free
is not a process of "thinking"
but an immediate and all-inclusive
Discovery.
It is instantaneous
this Awakening to Freedom
on the thrill
of our Inner Recognition.

*T*o know True Freedom,
is not to know one is merely free,
but to know one *is* Freedom,
Itself.

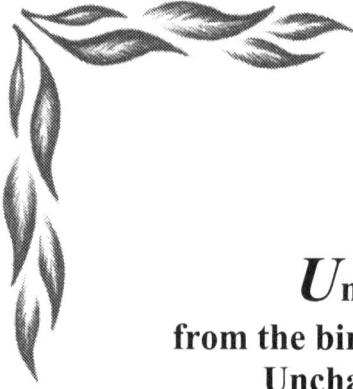

*U*ntie thyself
from the binding stake of fear.
Unchain the heart
from any idea that the Actual,
the Omnipresent Goodness,
is missing from anything in the earth.
There is no mixture of good and evil
within the shadow system about us.
Fearlessness ---
sees only the cause of the material,
the Spirit,
the Soul Reality,
in and behind the *apparent*.
If this is clear,
we need not fear
the symbolic evidence
of manifest conditions;
those,
which in Truth,
only *seem* to exist.

*I*f God is everywhere present
then that which is called evil
is nowhere present.
Evil is not Reality,
nor is it's result.
What is this that appears as
one nation striking another?
In Reality, it never happened!
Spirit knows nothing about
humanity's ignorance of Unity,
or the *action* that succeeds it.
As long as we look to the world,
to its appearances of evil and hatred,
we shall forever be baffled.
"All that is seen exists not at all."
We are but shadows,
the outer play of Spirit,
in an illusionary drama,
staged for the education
of
Soul.

*E*vil is a manifestation,
not Reality.
Let not,
that which *is not,*
weave a way
into the arena of attention.
There is nothing to be against,
there is no evil to reject.
Why put attention on something
which in Truth
had no Reality
to begin with?

*W*hy, man, should ye fight at all?
For illusionary victories
in a transient world?
Knowing the indestructible,
how can one not have certainty?
Soul cannot slay,
nor can it be slain.
True Victory is already ours.

*I*f one believes in Perfection,
there is not even this statement
to question.
This being:
Knowing God is All,
there can be no effect,
but Itself.

*T*he *S*tars
follow the guidance
of a Supernal Force.
See the Perfection,
follow their course.

"I"

the Principle of Creation,
working as the Consciousness of the Universe,
moving through the stillness of the unconditioned,
as the *Divine Dreamer* of all that IS,
must,
as necessity of *My Law,*
not only set up the necessary conditions through,
which "I," the God of your Being,
will find expression,
as experience,
through the *experiencer*,
but to come forth as the nature
of the *experiencer itself,*
to be, as Myself,
all of which my subtle essence IS:
The Source, The Harmony, The Light,
and You Are That.

*W*hat you see, feel, touch and hear
is God experiencing Itself.
The Experiencer,
and what is Experienced,
are *at once*
the same Thing.

*O*ne needs to be aware
that *you are,*
and have always *been,*
the director, the creator,
of the movie you find yourself within.
As Spirit,
you are the "light" in the projector.
As Mind,
you are the director of the "film."
As Thought,
you are the creator of time,
the "screen" upon which
the movie plays.
All this movie consists of
is the pulse of animation,
a visually enchanting dance,
of atoms.

*U*ndaunted,
"I" am the watcher
of this passing show.
Trouble me not
this world of appearances;
for it is *"I"* that have permanence.

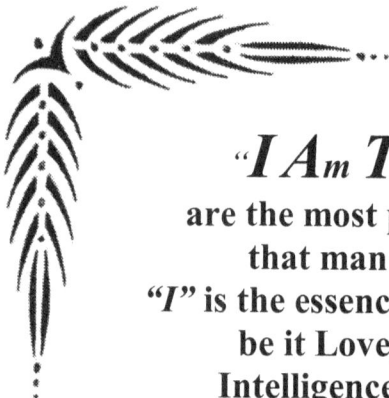

"I Am That I Am"
are the most powerful words
that man can speak.
"I" is the essence of the Universe;
be it Love, Harmony,
Intelligence or Serenity,
it is the True identity
of the individual as Spirit,
the absolute Fact of man's Being.
"AM" is the asserting factor,
the awareness and certainty of this Fact
existing in man.
"AM" embraces the essence through
Conscious Recognition,
which,
in turn,
brings forth
That,
which the essence *is.*
Through a Realization
of the transcendent meaning
of the these words,
and the humble proclamation thereof,
one can embody all of
That,
which,
God Is.

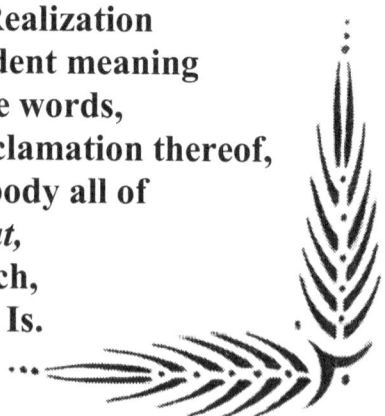

*I*f one is to label the object of his search,
be it God, Love or Truth,
he is placing it outside of himself.
In doing so,
one is forever seeking to *reach*
the object of his desire.
Yet there is no entity apart
from the thing being labeled,
no object of desire,
apart from thy Self.
Therefore,
seek not any object,
label not any thing,
but bind The Reality unto thy Self,
in Eternal Recognition of
what IS,
through the Eternal Proclamation of
I AM.

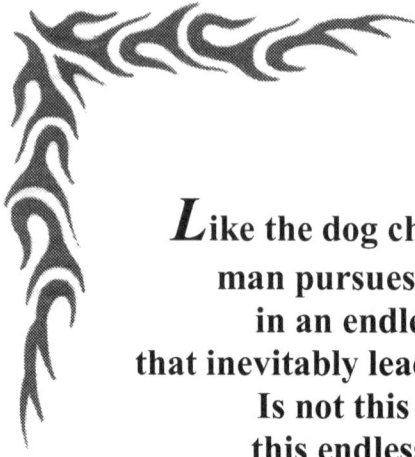

*L*ike the dog chasing it's tail,
man pursues his desires
in an endless circle
that inevitably leads him nowhere.
Is not this chasing,
this endless seeking
of gratification,
of attainment,
entirely beside the point?
Is it not that we have neglected
the main issue ---
That God is the inherent fact
of man's being?(5)
To accept this fact is to know freedom;
freedom
from all distractive processes
that are less than the fact,
thereby
putting an end to
all illusionary desire,
the folly of becoming something
we are not *already*.

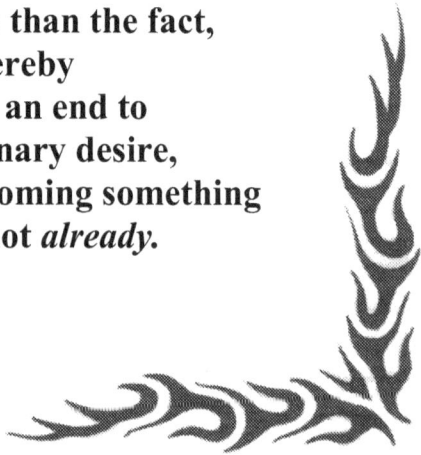

*G*odhood
is not a
becoming,
but an Awakening to
That
which has always
Been.
A continuous Realization
of greater
and greater
aspects of what
Already IS.

*A*ll processes to overcome conflict,
create more conflict.
Processes involve an element of time;
that of responses,
judgment,
and interpretation
which strengthen one's identification
with the conflict.
Liberation from conflict is
neither a process of determination,
discipline or will,
but an instantaneous arrival
within a moment
of victorious surrender
to your imagined sense of differences.

*I*n order for there to be judgment,
there must be a sense of
separation
from the object being judged.
This is illusion.

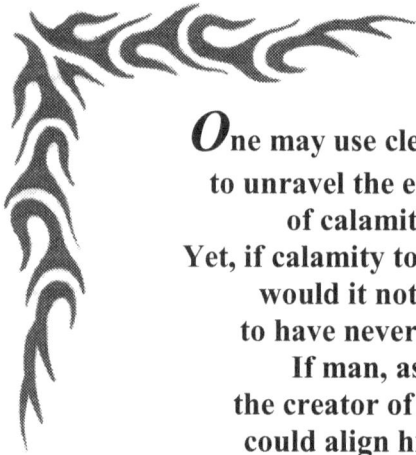

*O*ne may use clever techniques
to unravel the entanglements
of calamity's web.
Yet, if calamity touches your life,
would it not be better
to have never come to it?
If man, as Mind,
the creator of experience,
could align his thoughts
with the Unburdened Spirit,
if he were in league
with this Universal Solvent,
then calamity would have no point of origin.
Why? Because thought is the willing agent
to which *Spirit* faithfully responds.
All conditions are subservient to It ---
for the building blocks
of It's Creative Essence are
pre-existent
to all physical, mental, and material experience.
Spirit *awaits* your thoughts,
your choices,
to be made visible
in this self-created world.
Out in *front* of all experience,
ahead of all manifest characteristics,
Spiritual Thinking,
like a celestial wind,
cuts a swath before you,
laying aside anything that is unlike
Spirit,
Itself.

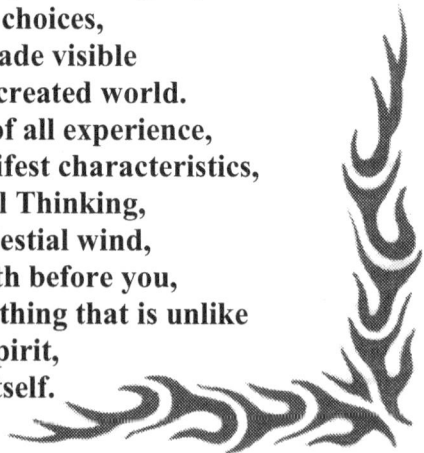

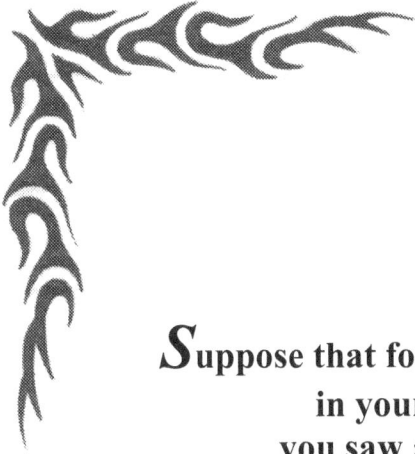

*S*uppose that for the first time
in your life
you saw an egg.
Understandably, to you, the egg
would seem "weird," "strange."
Yet if I were to explain to you,
completely,
the history of the "egg,"
you would understand.
If you ever hear the words
"weird" or "strange"
you can be certain that the
individual
from which they were spoken
is merely experiencing a lack
of understanding.

*T*here is no such thing as
Right or *Wrong,*
Good or *Bad,*
This or *That.*
No object of perception,
whether internal beliefs or
external manifestations,
are anything
in and of themselves.
What *is*, simply IS.
It is the "idea about"
what one perceives
that leads the perceiver
to believe
in such a possibility
of differences.

*T*here is no insanity,
schizophrenia,
or retardation
in all the world,
only the unintentional acquisition of
different states,
within a *single Consciousness.*
Those who consider the above descriptions
to be *Realities* in themselves
must find
they are nothing more than
convenient labels
to describe their misunderstanding of
Reality.

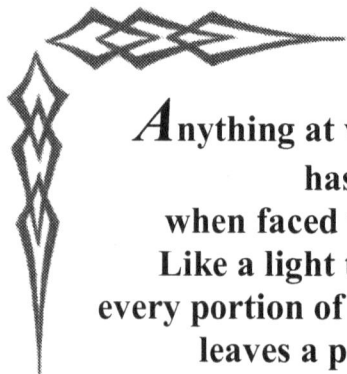

*A*nything at variance with the truth
has no potency
when faced with the Truth Itself.
Like a light that dispels darkness,
every portion of Truth that man discerns,
leaves a portion of falsehood
to fall away.
Look to this similarity in mathematics:
two plus two does not equal three,
nor does it equal five or six.
Once the true and indisputable
end of this equation (four) is reached,
the falsehood of any other number
is eliminated, set aside, forgotten.
Like the logic used in solving
any mathematical equation,
man may break down the enclosing structures
of his acquired perceptions and,
in turn,
remove all obstacles from his ascending path.
One by one he may peel away
the dark layers of what is not;
the decaying accumulation of suggestibility,
and bring himself closer to the Light;
the Ageless Clarity of what IS.
This is a way to Deliverance,
to departure,
a flawless way,
to Liberation.

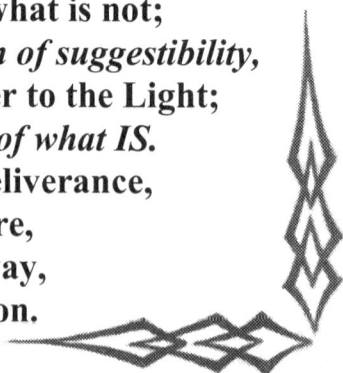

Disease is pronounced Dis-Ease. It is the outpicturing of inharmonious thought and the accumulated wreckage of false belief. This is the only birthing place from which the "appearance", disease, can have it's origin. Dis-Harmony is the Mother of Dis-Ease, the unsettling turmoil that stifles and strangles the channel for the Free Expression of Spirit. If one clearly sees that Dis-Ease is the result of one's thinking, then surely it will dissolve by changing that which created it. Dis-Ease needs no cure, for there is nothing *to* cure save one's Thinking, one's Realization, the certainty that if God, As Spirit is All, there can be no opposition to It. If God is All, where can disease and it's cause be found? You see, when the Truth is Known, when the mind can conceive of no opposite to It, then the Truth will annihilate anything less than the Truth Itself. When there is nothing left to support an "appearance" claim to Reality, then the illusion must, by Law, leave the mind and, in turn, the body. Harmonious thought then returns. Former beliefs slip away and the channel is cleared to the free flow of the Perfecting Spirit. Knowing this Truth, so-called germs and disease cannot touch one. Such appearances find no lodging place in the Body Devine, the Spirit Body within man, that shines through his Illuminated Consciousness, burning away all forms of disharmony.

*M*an struggles
to change his outer nature
according to his beliefs
of how it "should be."
Yet his nature is the result
of what he has believed
himself "to be."
There need not be change
through struggle,
for unknowingly,
it is *beliefs themselves*
that man struggles against.

*T*here is nothing in the world
that punishes one to suffering
save the limited beliefs
that one holds to be true.

*L*ife is *G*od ---
It does not,
cannot,
punish itself.
"You reap as you sow."
"It is done unto you as you believe."
This is not punishment,
but the law of
your own decree.

*C*ollectively, it is man's thinking
that shapes the world.
If we desire to change it,
we need only change
our thinking,
in regard *to* it.

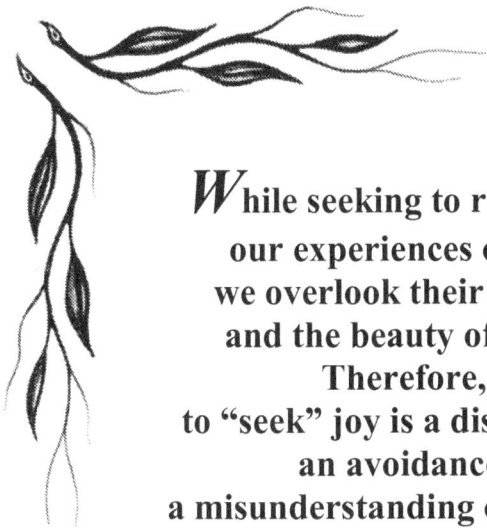

*W*hile seeking to recapture
our experiences of joy,
we overlook their source
and the beauty of Now.
Therefore,
to "seek" joy is a distraction,
an avoidance,
a misunderstanding of what *is.*
The joy you experienced
as the glory of yesterday's sunset
was a reflection,
a revealing glimpse
into the origin of
Eternal Beauty.
The sunset
the joy
the beauty
were never *apart* from you.
They are, in Actuality,
a spontaneous intimation,
an intuitive inner identification,
as the *remembrance*
of what *is,*
Yourself.

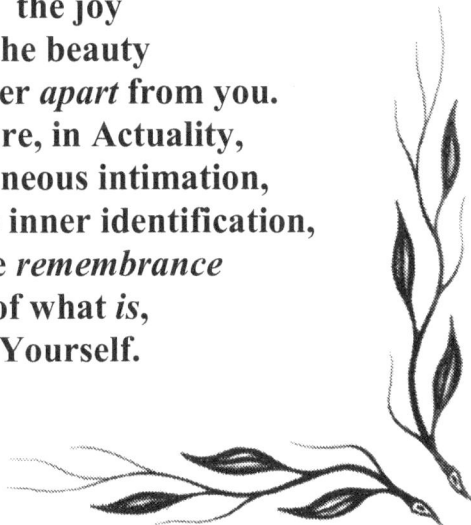

*T*he Complete,
the Already-in-Existence,
needs only our Recognition
to solidify as *Reality*
to the onlooker.
All that is seen as the manifest,
was brought forth
through the power
of Mind.
Man knows it not,
but *as* the One Mind,
drawing on the Subtle Essence,
he is Creator,
of the Phenomenal World.

*S*oul, as Spirit, was not born.
It had no beginning.
Nothing can be born
without an element of time;
time cannot Be without relation to objects.
Soul is timeless,
an *invisible Reality*.
From this premise it may be understood
that all that truly exists,
all that truly remains,
is the indestructible,
deathless and eternal Soul.
That which always *Was*
and will forever *Be*.

*T*here need be no mediator
between man
and
The Eternal;
for man is at once
Human and Divine.
The Door to Eternity lies in
man's Consciousness,
a Transcending Realization
that he is both
the One who knocks
and
the One who opens the Door.(1)

*T*he Eternal Truth cannot be denied.
You are everything God IS.
Whether you know this
or not
will never
change the fact
that *you* ARE.

*H*umanity's idea of space and time
have been a barrier to the experience
of Reality.
However, fortunately, such ideas
can be obliterated.
In the meditative state,
merging into the Omnipresent,
one is left without an *individual perspective*,
a point of reference,
from which to "view" or "measure"
space and time.
Such a one, no longer *looking outward*
from a *singular point of consciousness*,
has become immersed in the
Simultaneous All Pervasive,
the Everything Everywhere.
Here, then, space and time become relative,
they disappear.
One must contemplate the importance of this,
for now, consciousness may penetrate
the Cosmic,
transcending the limits of time,
and the confines of the
three dimensional world.

*T*here is no element of "time"
in Spiritual Reality.
Consciousness exists everywhere
in the Universe
simultaneously.
One does not *travel*
to any given point
within the Universe;
for you,
as Consciousness,
are *already there.*

*T*he unencumbered and uncontaminated
Realms of God
are identical with the Inner Reality
of man.
HERE time is unnecessary,
for there can be nothing left to "learn"
where all *is* Known.
HERE, time is unimaginable,
for there can be nothing to "improve"
where all *is* Perfect.
HERE, time is meaningless,
for there can be nothing to "measure"
where all *is* Boundless.
HERE, time serves no purpose,
for there can be nothing to "do"
where all *is* Complete.
HERE, time is non-existent,
for there can be nothing to "become"
where all *is* Finished.

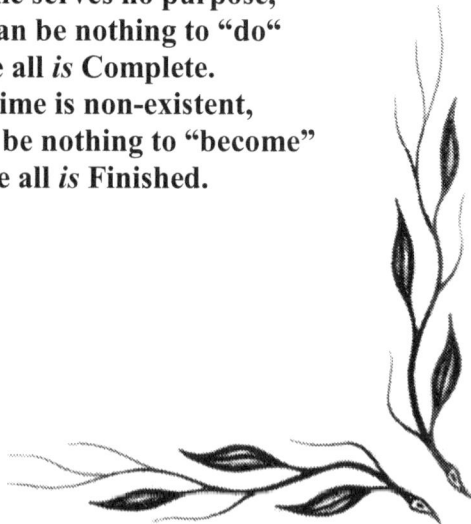

*T*he seeker of Divine Illumination
felt he needed time
to reach his destination.
Yet, the seeker came to find
that his efforts in time
had only prolonged his Realization
that *he was* the Destination.

*A*toms, the building blocks of the Universe,
are the *Living Truth* ---
that of which all things are composed.
Each endowed with Intelligence,
they respond to *Thought* ---
the glue,
the cohesive element to which they gather,
manifesting into being,
crystalizing into materiality,
for the apprehension
of the external senses.

*A*ll movement and form
is but the dance of
Atoms,
stimulated by
the electronic framework of
Thought Patterns
appearing upon the
screen of time,
for the contemplation of
Soul.

"*T*hy *K*ingdom is *W*ithin."
How clear was His direction!
One need not *go* to the mountaintop,
the cave or cathedral,
to encompass the plans of God.
The Truth is where you are.
The sanctuary of the Temple,
the open gates to Revelation,
lie within the stillness
of thy *Self,*
the True Church,
thou has never left.

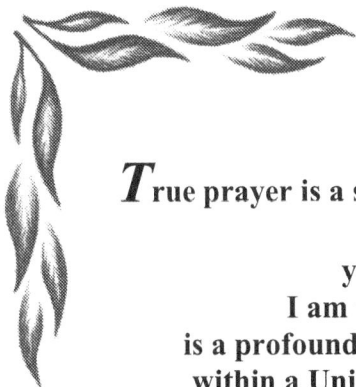

*T*rue prayer is a silent Realization of what,
in fact,
you ARE.
I am the All *in* All
is a profound Discovery that You,
within a Unity of Consciousness,
are the Universe of God.
The basis of everything within this Universe
is Consciousness ---
that which transcends both space and time.
Everything It is,
is in the same instant, the same thing,
here, there, and everywhere.
You, as Consciousness, are the Universe.
The Universe, as Consciousness, is You.
There never was, nor will there every be,
anything outside *Yourself.*
"Thy Kingdom is Within."
"The body of thy Conscious Universe is thy Self."
When one comprehends this,
when one truly *Knows,*
then prayer, in the traditional sense,
looses it's significance.
One comes to the Realization
that there is nothing to pray *for,*
save the compassionate desire for all humanity
to also *Know* that everything the Universe of God is,
is That,
which,
We Are.

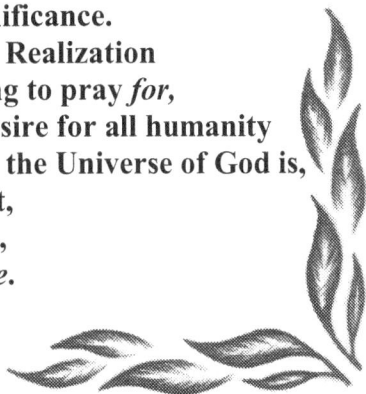

Self is not the receiver
of Divine Wisdom.
Self is that Wisdom
of which Wisdom is drawn.

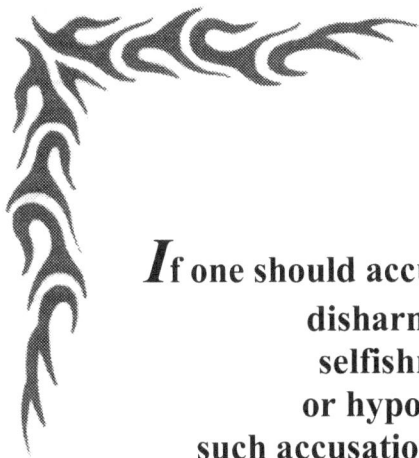

*I*f one should accuse the world of
disharmony,
selfishness,
or hypocrisy,
such accusations would be,
in essence,
against the shadows wrought
of his own unconscious believing.
Through clear reasoning of what *is*,
by the elimination of what is *not*,
one would find
that these pretentious formulations
could only have arisen
as subjective misinterpretations of the Truth.
Such shadows are the result of
your own unconscious trait of character;
they are but reflections to their Creator
--- You,
offering blameless opportunity
for their transcendence.

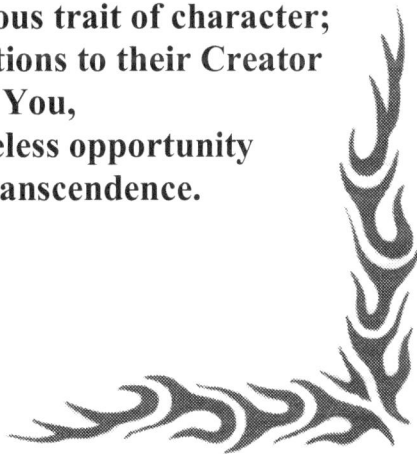

*O*ne will find
that behind every "supposed"
negative experience,
that its *Cause* arose
from discordant thinking.
To find such *Cause*,
is to find
Keys to your freedom.

*T*hrough belief
in the struggle about him,
man perpetuates such delusion.
To see only *One*
he ends that illusion.

*F*or one to say:
"I believe in this"
Is to say:
"I do not believe in that"
This is dangerous.
For to agree with one thing
is to disregard another.
In so doing,
one removes oneself
from other possibilities
within a Reality
one has not yet fathomed.

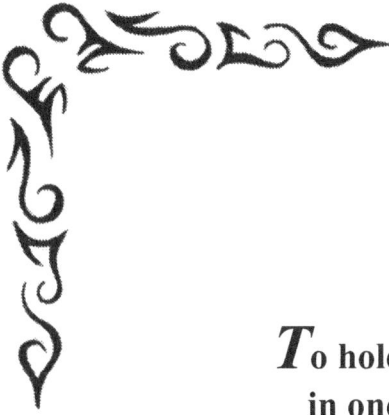

*T*o hold a belief
in one thing
is to deny whatever opposes that belief.
Unknowingly,
such a believer
has removed himself
from the variance
of potential awaiting
in the unrealized.
To be without beliefs
is to be open
to the possibilities
of new Discovery,
that latent potential within the overlooked,
the blooming Awareness
of that which IS.

*T*ime is not a necessity
to become or arrive
at some illusive destination.
Completion,
the end of all struggle to attain,
can be Realized
in a single flash of Inner Recognition.
Once one arrives at such Realization,
one sees that time
was never contingent
upon one's arrival.

*W*hen illumination dawns
on Consciousness,
one realizes he had always
Known.
The only difference being,
heretofore,
is he did not know,
he Knew.

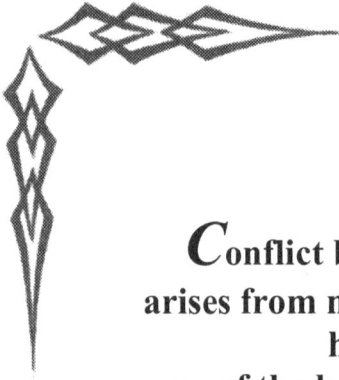

*C*onflict between individuals
arises from man's self-importance,
his defense
of the beliefs he clings to.
However,
can it matter what another believes
if you have seen beyond them?
The Realization of an Unalterable Reality
extinguishes one's reaction to any belief
that is less than
The Realization.
Therefore,
look only to this Universal Solvent,
the *Sameness* behind the clash
of conflicting beliefs.
For it will be found
that within such *Realization*
one is left without a lesser position to defend,
and consequently,
nothing,
to conflict against.

***T*he *L*aw of the *U*niverse**
is as exacting as mathematics.
All that is given
is free to return,
thus liberating man
from his sense of need.
Given freely, then,
must surely be,
in itself,
a path to Freedom.

*I*f you seek love,
give love.
It will return
as surely
as it was sent.
Knowing this Law
of Receiving,
one will no longer *seek love*,
but know
that it's Source,
lies *within*.

*I*s it not because of so much seeking,
so much effort
in the search,
that we do not find,
that we do not see,
what is Here and Now.
We are as foolish
as the man
trying to catch the wind
in the palm of his hand.
That which you desire
is *already* yours.
Lose the need to *get*
and you will discover,
the world cannot give you
what you already *have*.

*L*ove, as *L*ife, is the desire to be,
to experience and to express.
Love, *as* all things, is continually
Awakening *through* All things.
It is creating Itself *in each instant*
through a Realization of Itself,
and in the very *same instant*,
the very *same Realization*
is taking place within the thing Created.
Love, as Creation, are United in *one* Awareness,
one Life, *one* Consciousness……expressing.
The timeless and "invisible" Life of Love
projects outward *from* Itself,
then back *upon* Itself.
In a perpetual process of Self-Recognition,
Self-Awakening and Self-Sustainment,
love solidifies as matter,
becoming more and more of that
which It is Knowing Itself to be.

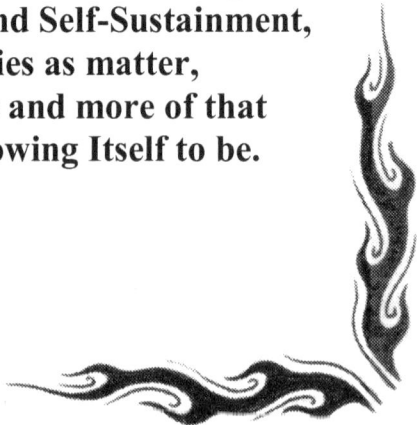

Does the bird stop it's flight in depression
when the fish escapes it's grasp?
Does the cat bemoan it's fate
when the mouse gets away?
Of course not.
They are not burdened
by a consideration of failure.
They do not look back
to contemplate what has been.
Animals can be wiser than humans,
their attention is in the moment,
their Spirit is fixed on opportunity,
on assurance,
provided in the everlasting
Now.

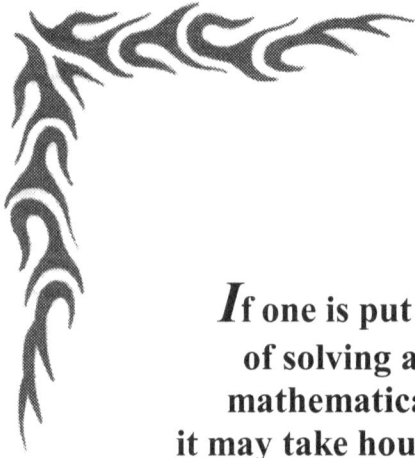

*I*f one is put to the task
of solving a complex
mathematical formula
it may take hours, even days.
Yet once the end of the
equation is reached
one may realize that the "answer"
had always existed.
Simply put, the conscious mind
had yet to "discover"
the end calculation.
This is true with what every individual
has yet to know,
For nothing *new* is ever perceived;
it only *seems so*
as the consciousness of "Now"
comes into apprehension
of what *already exists*.

*R*egarding the *S*elf *E*xistent *T*ruth.
Eventually, all things will reach
the same Final Conclusion.
It is appropriate that this be so,
for there is but *One Truth*,
there is but *One conclusion*
to be reached.
It could not be otherwise.

What strange imagination of man
to think that God
sent evil into the world
for Its creations to overcome;
to leave us with the idea
that there *is* something
to overcome.
If evil was *nothing* to begin with,
if in fact it had no beginning,
then it remains nothing
but the phantoms
of strange imagination.

*T*he One Law
brings forth
the "appearance"
of either Good or Bad.
Yet there is but One Force
that knows only to respond,
to work,
always in accord
with the thought behind It.
Evil and disharmony
are not things in themselves,
but miscreations
of man's
erroneous thinking.

*A*ll one sees as disharmony
is the outpicturing
of ill conceived thoughts
and ideas
held within the collective consciousness
of
world beliefs.

*M*an foolishly creates
the undesirable conditions
that surround him.
Then,
believing them to be Real,
goes to battle
against the shadows
of his own creation.

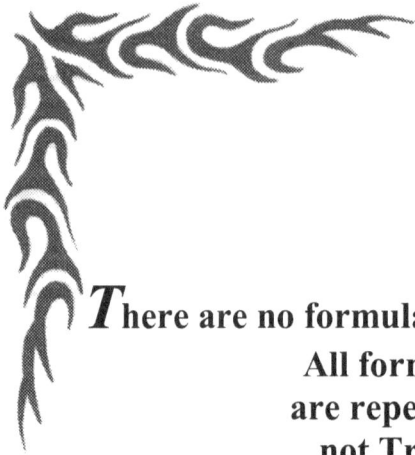

*T*here are no formulas to Self-discovery.
All formulas
are repetition,
not Truth.
The discovery of the Self
is unique to each individual;
it cannot be taught,
it can only be caught.(4)
Therefore,
forget beliefs,
forget books,
forget teachings,
forget everything;
for it is only in a state
in which one knows Nothing,
will one comprehend
That,
which is above all analytical thinking.

*I*f one has no "goal" of Attainment,
all thoughts,
formerly toward that endeavor,
would turn within.
All thoughts of becoming,
that had crowded the mind,
would then be dissipated.
No longer seeking outside itself,
the mind becomes still,
open,
and receptive,
leaving room for
the Entrance
of the Divine.

*W*ith attention held steadfast
to the willing executive
of God's presence,
Spirit,
the Inner Angel,
begins to invigorate and glow
through the external frame
of man.
Just as the chill of winter must give way
to the warming sun of summer
the movement
of the Angels inner alchemy
sheds forth
it's illuminating rays,
slowly,
yet always surely,
to the outer expression
of Life Divine.

*T*he negative
always
reflects the opposite.
Once the Truth is recognized,
there is no need
to look back upon Its shadow.
The negative
is only a tool
used
for the recognition of Truth,
then forgotten.

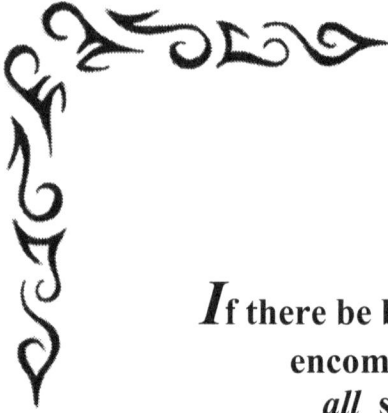

*I*f there be but *One* thing
encompassing
all space,
how can something
other
be derived from it?
If pie be smashed
into a billion pieces,
the pieces remain pie.
All that came from a
single Thing
can be nothing other
than the
Thing itself.
You see,
it is impossible
to *not* be That
which God is.

*T*here is but one sin in the world.
That is:
Ignorance that All is God.
Therefore, it follows;
that sin would vanish altogether
if this Truth be Known.

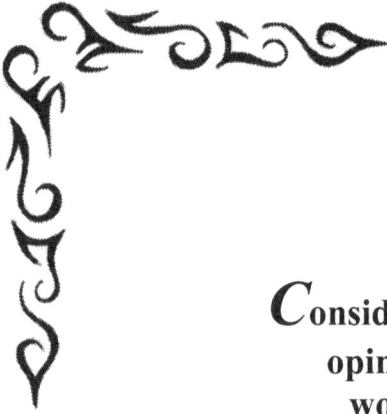

*C*onsiderations,
opinions,
words
and descriptions
about the world,
in fact,
the Universe,
mean nothing when observed
in the *Whole of Truth*.
When all is in Unity,
which it IS,
then all becomes nameless,
beyond description,
beyond opinion.
When all blends into One,
when words and translations cease,
That is Reality ---
That is God.

*I*s not all life, God's life?
How proud can one be
when this Truth is Known?
Let go of such pride,
such vain illusion.

*B*eyond man's limited senses,
God reveals Itself as It IS,
through the Celestial aspects
of *what* It IS.
Without the aid of the outer ears
one hears That, the Logos,
as the Song Eternal.
Without the aid of the outer eyes
one sees That, the Fiery Light,
as the Elliptic Flame of
Love Divine.

*B*efore the world was,
the Heavens and all things within
Knew.
Quietly, they have forever
proclaimed their Unity
in the Harmony of
Beingness.
They sing of perpetual birth,
of timeless eternity,
and unspeakable
Majesty.

*C*ause and *E*ffect,
Positive and Negative,
may be opposing forces.
But in the final analysis
they are found to be
two sides of a Unitary Principle.
Together,
they move upon one another
to bring into manifestation
all manner of Creation.
Just as summer and winter
are essential
for the harmony and growth
of vegetation,
they are not separate,
but two phases,
of a *Single Nature.*

*N*ature,
in all its subtle awareness,
already Knows.
When one comes to *know* nature,
as *It Is*,
one falls into harmony,
with *It.*

*T*hought, as energy, does not dissipate.
Every thought
that has ever *been* thought
lives "*Now,*"
in the matrix
of collective consciousness.
All,
then,
that *can* be Known,
is "*there*" to *be* Known,
when the mind is
clear, open, still
and
receptive.

*S*o-called telepathy is simple.
Thoughts
are tangible *things*
that float
through the ethers,
to the receptive consciousness
of all men.

*A*ll Wisdom,
is that Wisdom,
coming to Know,
Itself.

*F*rom the chirping of the cricket,
to the instant a leaf is loosened
from the branch of it's origin,
there is a reason,
a synchronistic harmony of order,
behind all things of nature.
Though the infant
is brought forth from the womb
to breathe but a few breaths,
a *soul,*
inhabited that tiny body briefly,
intentionally,
not only for experience
through the exacting order
of *it's* eternal best interest,
but in accordance with the necessity
to perfect the temperament
of it's *mother's soul.*
Grieve not for what seems unintentional,
accidental or unjustified;
for there is nothing taking place,
within this world,
without a purposeful cause
to which it is due.

*D*welling in the realms beyond,
Soul, contemplates Its Noble Aspirations,
only those which are advantageous
for Its future growth,
Its future advancement,
upon the ladder of Ascension.
Fearlessly, Soul enters this world,
aware, and in agreement
with the hardships It will face.
As Soul, we *chose* this life.
Our trials,
our seemingly troublesome
yet necessary paths
temper and hone the Soul;
they mellow us, as we awaken,
to the Sacred Qualities of God.
Therefore,
let us face this life with bravery,
with responsibility and dignity.
For it would be foolish
to bemoan the hardships
of our pre-ordained Destiny,
the path we chose,
the path we entered upon,
Knowingly.

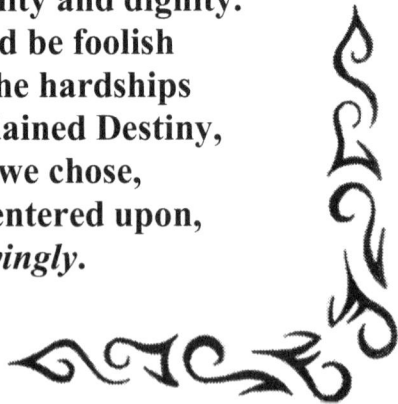

*Y*ou cannot go through
the gates of Grace
without first having experienced
discouragement.
If the past has brought you sadness,
be thankful for the lesson therein;
for life is never what happens
to you,
but always what happens
for you.

*T*he Mind of God
realizes greater aspects
of Itself
through the outlets
of that same Mind
awakening in man.
Our realization of It,
is in the same instant,
Its joyous realization,
of Itself.

*I*f you comprehend
and hold to the Realization that
the Perceiver *is* the Perceived,
the Perceived *is* the Perceiver;
the Seer *is* the Seen,
the Seen *is* the Seer;
the Belief *is* the Believer,
the Believer *is* the Belief;
the Knower *is* the Known,
the Known *is* the Knower;
the Experiencer *is* the Experienced,
the Experienced *is* the Experiencer;
the Thinker *is* the Thought,
the Thought *is* the Thinker.
You are now O*ne*,
with *Creation*.

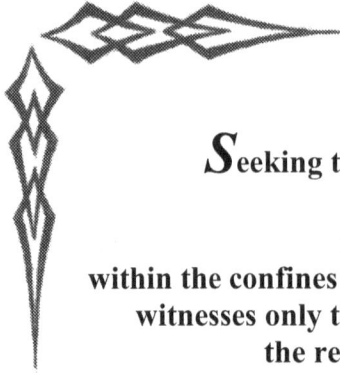

*S*eeking the Luminous Reality,
mind,
entrapped,
within the confines of it's own encasing structure,
witnesses only that which it has created ---
the reflections of itself.
If this is so, can the human mind grasp
that which it perceives as beyond itself?
Is it possible for the finite mind
to apprehend the infinitude of God?
This enigma is solved when man,
as mind,
through "effortless effort"
finds the Silence,
the All Prevailing Stillness of Reality,
within the tranquility of *its* center.
Here, in a glance,
mind peeks through the opening Door
to glimpse the unrestricted Luminosity
of its true Spiritual and Infinite nature.
Only a glimpse is sufficient
to "see" the vastness of Eternity
through the Door
of its once enclosed structure.
It is enough for Mind,
which was once finite,
to discover the Immeasurable,
to Enter That,
which *is* Infinitude,
Itself.

*T*here is nothing
that constitutes
any difference between individuals,
save the degree of Realization
to the Divinity they Are.
One may Know what, in fact, he IS;
the other has yet to discover It.
That is all the difference there is.

*M*an,
as Spirit,
has entrapped himself within this world,
through his forgetfulness
of the Spirit he is.
Once man wanders through this world of duality,
to again discover
the Singular Nature of Spirit,
never again will he need to manifest,
within the shadow worlds of Creation,
but is again free to roam
the plains of Pure Existence.

*I*f one sees the *Infinite*
concealed within,
he then can tell;
he must crack the egg
and eliminate the shell.

*W*hen one knows the *C*reative *P*rocess;
how things come into Being,
one naturally knows
how they dissolve.
Reverse the Process ---
"Return Unto Me."

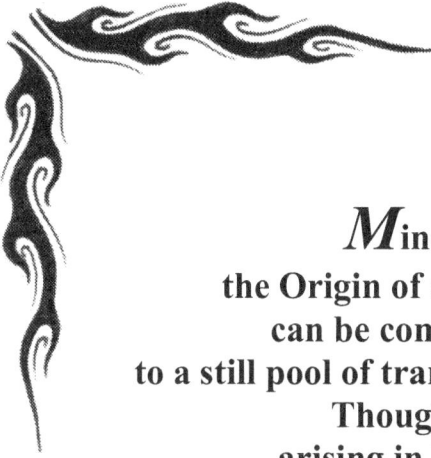

*M*ind,
the Origin of all that *is*,
can be compared
to a still pool of transparent water.
Thought,
arising in Mind,
can be compared
to a pebble dropped within this pool,
the ripples therefrom
can be seen, counted and measured.(4)
From this example,
it may be comprehended that
from the Invisible,
arises the visible;
from the Unmeasurable
arises the measurable;
from the Timeless
arises time;
from the Motionless
arises motion;
from the Uncreated
arises creation.

*M*an's seeming problems
and difficulties
could be eliminated
if he were to relinquish memory
as a platform for their resolution.
Regardless of their re-appearance,
seeming problems are always *new*.
They cannot be approached
by a mind that is tethered
to the past,
the repetition of the *old*.
The resolutions you seek
are always found
in the *moment* ---
the moment you LOOK
without comparisons,
without the interposing of ideas,
theories or analyzation,
to what you believe
as the problem itself.

*A*ll processes to overcome internal conflict,
perpetuates such conflict.
Processes involve an element of time;
that of responses,
judgment,
and interpretation
which strengthens one's identification
with the conflict.
Liberation from conflict is
neither a process of determination, overcoming,
discipline or will,
but an instantaneous realization
that *all* internal conflict is
mind-imagined and self-created.
Surrender such imagination,
let it go,
for the only thing *to* overcome
is the "imagination"
that there *is something*
to overcome.

*R*elax.
Your life has never been out of order.
What should have been…..
Was.
Be still.
Your life can never fall out of order.
What ought to be…..
IS.
You can only *imagine* it…..
Otherwise.

*N*othing within this world can demonstrate
the power to hurt.
It is you,
through your *believing,*
who delegate power
to the seemingly effectual,
yet non-effectual negatives
born of imagination.
Unravel your strings of agreement,
through bold insistence,
that there is any power of demonstration,
save the Power within
the uncontaminated clarity
of your Original Believing.

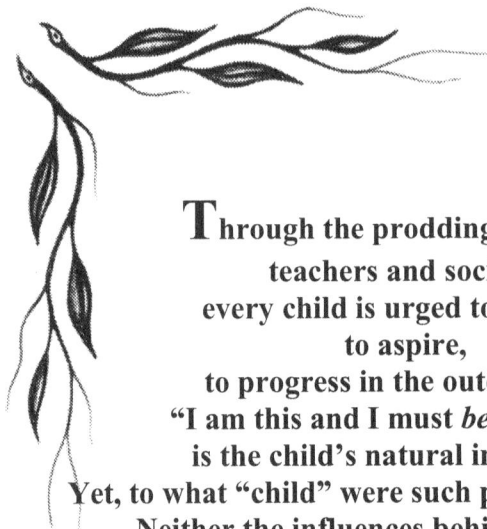

Through the prodding of family,
teachers and society,
every child is urged to achieve,
to aspire,
to progress in the outer world.
"I am this and I must *become* that,"
is the child's natural inclination.
Yet, to what "child" were such proddings directed?
Neither the influences behind the urging,
or the young recipient thereof,
has recognized the difference between
the outward *identity*
and the *Completed inward Entity.*
The child, without such wisdom,
unaware of his Real Nature,
comes to the suspicious feeling
it is "he himself," the delicate "me,"
that is somehow lacking,
insufficient and in need of change.
It is here that a distortion arises
within one's psychological nature.
Look deeply into this,
for it still effects you today.
Ask yourself, the Child Within:
What "You" were your contacts addressing?
Did they teach you the difference then?
Do *you* know the difference now?

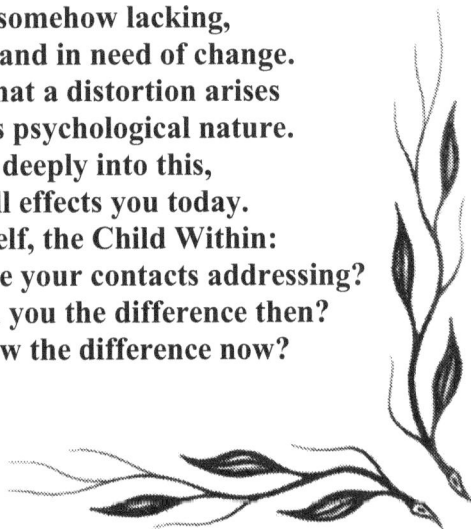

*S*tand firm
as the Lord of your environment.
Be not shaken
by *appearances* of adversity,
but react to *nothing*.
For it is by loosening your attention
on the things that can be shaken,
that those things that cannot,
may alone remain.

*M*any of man's struggles
are the result of insecurity,
that which stems from what he considers
an inward void.
Yet this void only *seems* as void
until one enters it.
What man believes as emptiness,
is in reality,
the Fullness of God,
the Still and Silent Embrace
of *Security Itself.*

*T*he sight of things
the way they *appear,*
leads to the belief
they must remain
as they *seem.*
The experience of poverty
and famine
within the regions of our world
are perpetuated,
by law,
through the innerlink
of such *collective* belief.
The sight of *lack* is a false
and disparaging claim
of its certainty to continue
to the minds of those
who observe it.
Such appearances of calamity
cannot be broken
by the Higher Vision of a few,
but only through
the Sighting of One,
by Many,
to the effect for All.

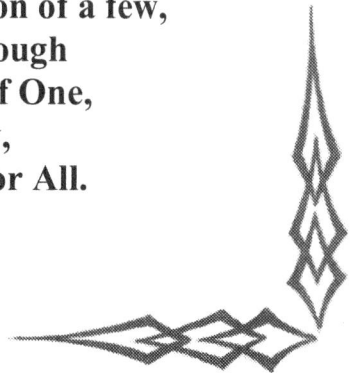

*A*ll that is perceived
by our limited senses
seem real,
look real,
yet are not *the* Real.
The world is an appearance,
a shadow cast
by the Reality behind it.
Just as a mirror reflects an object,
yet it is not *the* object
that it reflects.

*I*f you think your ideas
concerning Creation
are substantial,
resolve all back to *One*.
If it is not found there,
it is not the *Real*.

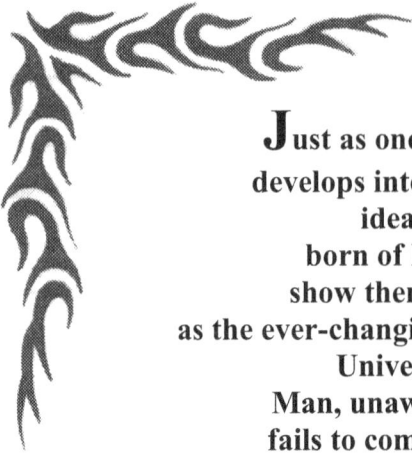

Just as one thought
develops into another,
ideas,
born of Mind,
show themselves
as the ever-changing phenomenal
Universe.
Man, unawakened,
fails to comprehend
this instantaneous flux,
this movement of Thought
within all component objects;
the continual modifying pulsation
of perpetual transformation.
All that is perceived
as *external nature,*
is,
in Realty,
*the inner crystalization of thought forms
in a labyrinth of inner connected ideas.*
Such inner connection can be likened
to the blending together
of many drops of water
to form a singular ocean.(4)
Mind, as thought,
existing as the manifest form of
phenomenal appearances
are those drops of water,
intermingled,
formulating and sustaining the Cosmos,
the Ocean of all Creation.

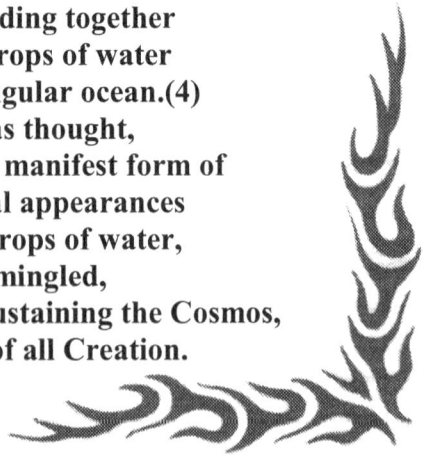

*I*t may take eons
to release us from
the Karmic debts of our past.
Such a foreboding task
may take lifetimes.
That is,
unless the collector
of the past,
the ego,
is no longer there
to receive the debt.

*K*arma,
punishment and condemnation,
are impossibilities
for the one who has dispelled
the illusion of time.
Reality exists only
in the moment.
The past is obliterated;
it is nothing but a shadow,
cast by what went before.

*I*f one finds True Contentment
he speaks but little.
What is there to mention of the past?
It is gone.
What is there to say of the future?
It has not arrived.
And what is taking place in the moment?
It is so obvious,   so perfect,
there is no need for comment.

*I*f one is to know his Self
as the Divinity he IS,
then he should regard others
as the same.
Exalt Humanity
above their estimations.
For to see All,
as above the world,
is to be there also.

*R*ecognition of One Authority;
the beginning of world transformation,
from the dropping of formula and imitation,
to the birthing of the New Imagination ---
"I" am that authority.
Not I,
as you have known,
but "I"
the Creative Intelligence,
the Restorer of
that which is not,
to that which is to BE,
the Higher Reality of humanity,
above the world of
the repetitive mind.

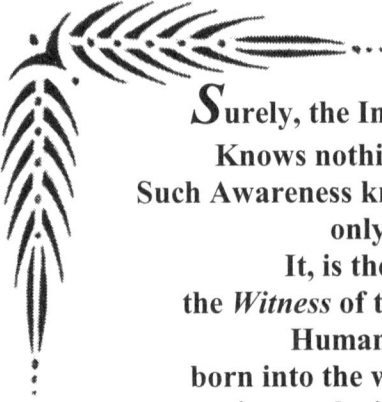

*S*urely, the Infinite Awareness
Knows nothing of suffering.
Such Awareness knows and experiences
only Itself.
It, is the *Watcher*,
the *Witness* of the human drama.
Humanity alone,
born into the world of manifest,
experiences the illusion of suffering,
an emotion that could never have arisen
by itself,
but only in relation *to something*;
our relation with the world
of events, people and things.
The transcendence of such emotion
comes through *Remembering* our
Infinite Nature.....
that which remains untouched,
undaunted by all
worldly experiences.
In *Remembering* it can be seen
that *nothing has changed*,
we still Are, and will always Be,
the Infinite Awareness.
As such, "we" never were our experiences,
"we" never were our emotions,
"we" never suffered,
but have forever remained
the untroubled *Watcher*,
the silent *Witness*,
behind the
human drama.

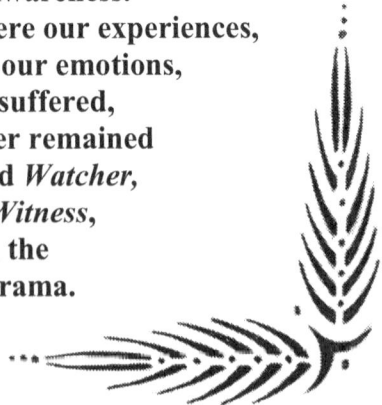

*W*hen one finds freedom
from the dim shadows of the past,
there can only be clarity forthcoming.
For it is the past,
moving through the present,
that shapes the future.

*R*eality leaves no "void" within man
from loved ones departing.
That which *seems* as a void
is merely a lack of recognition
to what is Truly There;
the stillness of God,
the essence to which all things
are returning.
Do not run from this seeming emptiness,
the Lover within is calling.
Embrace It and rest,
for *There* will be *found*,
all you have believed,
as *missing*.

*O*ne cannot fear the unknown;
fear can only be attributed
to the outcome of worldly Knowledge.
Is one born with fear when he knew God alone?
Or is fear the result
of what one has come to know?
One cannot fear death, the unknown;
one may "think" he fears death,
yet your very thinking is the result of Knowledge.
What one fears is really that of losing
a relationship with
all he *has* known.

*C*onsciousness pervades *Everything;*
the stars, planets, rocks and stones.
The very air you breathe
is conscious and alive.
The only difference between man
and such Creation
is that man has *Self* Consciousness,
the ability to comprehend
and *Know*,
that he is *One* with the above,
that which he,
as Conscious Creation,
IS.

*T*he seer and the seen
are the same Thing.
If one sees anything but God,
he does not know
what he is looking *with,*
or looking *at.*
"I see the Christ in every face,
in every form,"
is the acknowledgement
of the undeceived.

*C*ompletion is an established Universal Fact,
as above,
so it IS below.
The Transfiguration of man,
to Life Divine,
is not an achievement,
nor the result of invocation;
for if one's vision of the Absolute be fixed,
It is "done" unto him,
he need not invoke It's establishment.
To do so,
would be as if one
were to persuade the Universe
of what It already Knows
Itself
to Be.

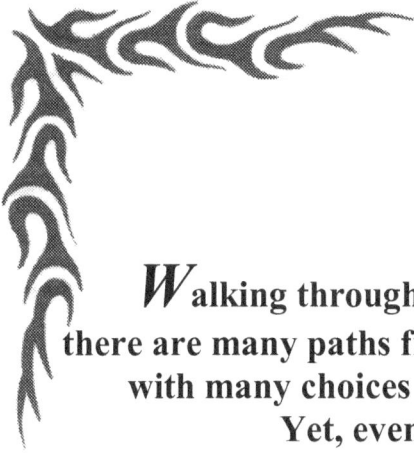

*W*alking through the Book of life
there are many paths from which to choose,
with many choices along each path.
Yet, eventually,
all choices,
all paths,
lead back to their point of origin....
all lead back
to the threshold
of the Author's Temple.
You see, the Cosmic Order of life is infallible.
Confidentially,
we need only live the story
that has already been told;
for there needn't be concern of error
in a world
where free will and predestination
co-exist.

*T*here is no injustice.
Awaken
from your dream of sorrow.
There is only *experience*
and what one believes
such *experience*
to be.

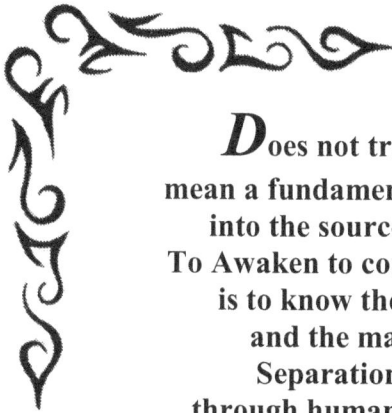

*D*oes not true forgiveness
mean a fundamental understanding
into the source of ignorance?
To Awaken to complete integration
is to know the One *is* many,
and the many *are* One.
Separation exists *only*
through human idea and belief.
These are the imaginary walls of isolation
which we have constructed between our
selves, societies, cultures and religions.
This is the source, the sleep of ignorance
which retards the true advancement of humanity.
If this is seen, do we need to blame,
then forgive, that which sleeps?
Can we hold our world responsible
for it's actions
while dreaming the dream of separation?
We should look *beyond* blame,
before any need of forgiveness arises;
for to do otherwise is but a waste of time.
It is us, you and me,
who must tear down
these superficial walls of ignorance
which we have all helped to erect.
It is *our* responsibility
to roll aside these dreams of separation,
to put away our isolating and deceptive beliefs,
then show forth, conclusively,
that only through love, born of Unity,
will come the Great Healing of Humanity.

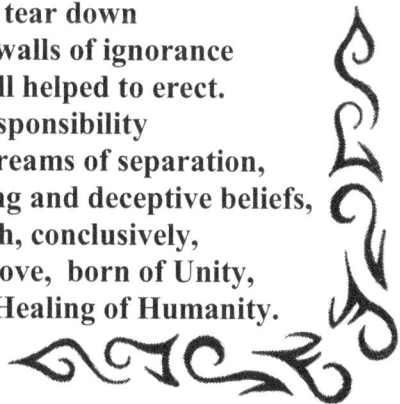

*A*ny effort
toward proving oneself to the world
is really an attempt
to convince oneself
of what he does not yet Know
himself to be.
However,
when one Realizes Completion,
where all is One,
where the world *is* as *himself*,
he then *Knows;*
there is nothing *to* prove,
nothing to prove anything *to*.

*T*his earth space in which we live is shared by the inhabitants of all plains of existence. We are not apart from the so-called living and dead, nor separated by dimensions of the so-called here and there. All realms of the invisible are Here and Now. If there be a separation, it is not through time and space, but through an atomic structure of frequency vibration. For example, as ice melts into water, as water evaporates into steam, and as steam becomes invisible, this is not an indication that steam is no longer here or no longer in existence. What has left our sight, has not left our space of habitation. Ice, water and steam all remain as the substratum of H_2O. Nothing has changed, save the form of it's atomic structure. Same atoms, same dimension, different frequency.

Beyond man's limited range of sensory detection of the elements are ghosts, angels and phantoms. At times these guests bleed through the dimensional frequencies we share. Although the course of vibration of the human eye can rarely see them (within the more intricate and finer structures of the Beauty Realms), they are as near us and just as authentic as the ground on which we stand.

*O*ur agreement with world,
as it is,
is the reason it appears,
as it does.
To the one who divorces himself
from
The Agreement,
the world still appears,
as it does,
yet now it is *seen*,
AS IT IS.

*Y*ou live within *your own* reality.
What you believe, IS.
What IS, is what you believe.
There is *nothing else* taking place.

*G*od and Man,
as one,
are
the Believing Mind,
the originator of the Cosmos.
Nothing can exist
independent of this Believer;
for the Believer gives existence
unto Itself,
and all things
It Believes.

*I*n the final analysis,
one will come to the Realization
that man
is not the experiencer of experience,
the seer of sights,
the thinker of thoughts,
the body moving,
the life living.
What man believes
as himself experiencing,
seeing,
thinking,
moving and living,
is not *himself* at all.
At the end of the Immaculate Conclusion,
one must find that there is *not man*,
but the All in All.
There is *only God*.

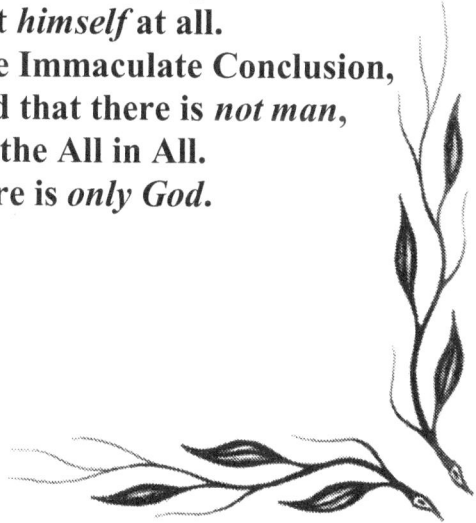

*W*hen the transformation comes,
when Illumination dawns
on the Consciousness of many,
the Transfiguration of the
Christ Mind will be revealed.
All men will then Know
the meaning of the Second Coming,
the Mystic Mirage of man to God.
Then, together, humanity will proclaim:
"I and the Father are One."

*P*ray to the *Self* of thyself
and proclaim from the standpoint
of the Eternal.
Speak from this,
your center of Certainty.
Do not ask --- Hoping
Command --- *Knowing*

*I*f my Will be Your Will,
then I am Love Itself,
provided with the opportunity,
through this recognition of Unity,
to do Your works further.

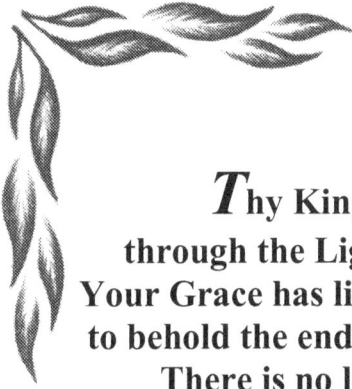

*T*hy Kingdom has come,
through the Light of Self-revelation.
Your Grace has lifted me above the world
to behold the end of this earthly journey.
There is no longer the necessity
to perpetuate this schooling
of manifest existence.
Yet, here I will tarry,
awaiting the transcendence,
while showered
in the Fiery Light of Your Celestial Flame.
You had been waiting behind the door
of my once slumbering mind.
Now Awake,
as triumphant and untellable benevolence,
words have lost all significance
within the stillness of the Sun
in your Majestic Eye.
Only the whisperings
of the Eternal Song
echo through the chambers of my heart,
enfolding me in the melody
of It's Everlasting,
Harmonious Embrace.

Sources

1. Holmes, Ernest. *Living the Science of Mind*, DeVorss Publications, 1980

2. Hopkins, Curtis Emma. *Scientific Christian Mental Practice*, DeVorss Publications, 1995

3. Krishnamurti, J. *The First and Last Freedom*, Harper Collins, 1975

4. Singh, Kirpal. *The Crown of Life*, Sawan Kirpal Publications, 1980.

5. Spalding, Baird T. *Life and Teaching of the Masters of the Far East*, Vol. No. 4, DeVorss Publications, 1976.

6. Twitchell, Paul. *The Flute of God*, IlluminatingWay Publishing, 1971.

Notes

Notes

Notes

Notes

Notes

www.ingramcontent.com/pod-product-compliance
Lightning Source LLC
Chambersburg PA
CBHW031257090426
42742CB00007B/495

9 7 8 0 6 1 5 1 5 6 1 6 3